Rich Like a Rothschild

*Jewish Humor From Poland Before
Nazi Germany's Holocaust*

Selection
Regina Gromacka

Art
Beata Kruk

Translation
Witold S. Kolankowski

Rich like a Rothschild

Authored by
Witold S Kolankowski

Illustrated by
Beatta Kruk

Copyright © 2011 Witold S. Kolankowski
All rights reserved.

ISBN-10: 0983906203
EAN-13: 9780983906209

Monument

This is a living monument to the memory of Polish Jews.

The Author

Witold Kolankowski was born in Latvia, and is a citizen of the United Kingdom. He worked in Warsaw in 1991-94 during Poland's transition from Communism to Democracy.

Hitler's response to the Warsaw Ghetto Uprising

Introduction

"Rich like a Rothschild" asks Jews what they would do if they were as rich as Baron Rothschild, the legendary financier whose daughters took piano lessons from Frederic Chopin.

I first read the Polish version of this book in Warsaw. It was the first collection of Jewish humor printed in democratic Poland since the collapse of Communism in 1989.

Jews were persecuted in Europe for centuries. Many fled to Poland, where they found freedom of worship. By 1850, more than three quarters of all Jews in the world lived inside the borders of old Poland. In some communities the dominant language was Yiddish. While preserving their own traditions, Polish Jews enriched the cultures of the world with scholars, writers, and great musicians such as Artur Rubinstein and Wanda Landowska. Many Polish Jews settled in the United States of America.

Hitler's Nazi Germany destroyed Poland's Jewish culture almost completely, and now only a few fragments remain. Yet, we are witnessing a revival of interest in that culture. A major Museum is being created, groups are forming for joint studies, Jewish schools are opening, and traditional Jewish restaurants are popular. Christian Poles and visitors from abroad are learning Hebrew, playing klezmer music, and studying Jewish history and literature.

Jewish humor is a bridge to the past. These jokes, dating to 19th century Tsarist Russia, may be the only Polish collection so far to be translated into English. Jewish humor was always popular in Poland and throughout the world, because its sharp wit is softened by warmth and wisdom. It makes us laugh while it reminds us that life has dangers which call for faith and spirit to survive another day. It makes fun of religion and free-thinking, oppression and survival, riches and poverty, war and marriage, and it does so without anger or malice. The world needs more of that. Jewish humor reflects the soul of Jewish people with their long history, religion and traditions, yet varies with the societies in which they lived. That is why the humor of Jews in Poland is special.

This book evokes the society and generation of people killed only because they were Polish Jews. They were murdered in Nazi death camps, and their ashes were dumped into unnamed pits. Yet, we can deny the Holocaust a total victory over these victims as long as we remember them, and their humor is the perfect monument to their memory. It recalls their loyalty to their ancient laws, their faith in their religion, their intelligence and sharp sense of business, their education, frugality and generosity. We see that they lived good lives, full of hope, even in times of injustice and oppression.

In Memory of Polish Jews

From the United States Holocaust Memorial Museum, Washington, DC.

"I have given the command, and I'll have anyone who utters but one word of criticism executed by a firing squad, that our war aim does not consist in reaching certain lines, but in the physical destruction of the enemy. Accordingly, I have placed my death-head formations in the east with orders to them to send to death mercilessly and without compassion men, women, and children of Polish derivation and language. Only thus shall we gain the living space (lebensraum) which we need."

This was Adolf Hitler's broadcast on August 22, 1939, 10 days before Germany invaded Poland, and launched World War II. Hitler was clear that it was Germany's objective and right to subject Poles to genocide, and the Jews were the first to be exterminated. This was the Holocaust in which close to three millions Polish Jews perished, mostly in Nazi death camps (A further three million Jews were killed in other occupied countries). Most of these victims are buried in unmarked mass graves.

The Germans tried to destroy every trace of their murders. Punishments for helping Jews were most severe in Poland, where those who helped Jews were hanged with their families in public squares. In spite of that, many Jews were hidden for 6 years by Christians.

Hitler created the Warsaw Ghetto to hold Polish Jews destined to die in his death camps. The last victims resisted in the Warsaw Ghetto Uprising of 1943. Nazi Germany's reply was total destruction of the Ghetto with its heroic Jews. A memorial monument was built while most of Warsaw still lay in ruins, but visitors must travel see it. This book is a memorial that can reach homes across the world. Jewish humor is a treasure of World Literature; it brings to life people who were our neighbors, who can be remembered as long as we can read.

Dedication

This book is dedicated to the heroes of the Warsaw Ghetto, to all Holocaust victims, and to all those who helped the Jews at the risk of death for themselves and their families.

1

Saints And Miracle Workers

Rabbis were religious teachers and leaders in Jewish communities. They were held in high esteem, especially by Chassidic Jews, who sometimes regarded them as holy men and miracle workers.

A young man comes to the rabbi for advice. Though his wife brought a very small dowry, he wants to start a business which would provide them with a good living.

"You are sure to succeed if you trade in bread or wood," says the rabbi. "The living will always need bread, and the dead will need wood for coffins. You can't fail."

The young man takes the rabbi's advice. He returns after a year as a bankrupt pauper, and says bitterly:

"Rabbi, you said that my business can't fail since the living will always need bread, and the dead will always need wood. But in our town they neither live nor die, they just wheel and deal."

✡ ✡ ✡

A Jewish community in Volhynia decides to pull down its crumbling old synagogue and build a new one. It soon becomes clear that they won't have enough money to finish the job. They are fifty thousand rubles short.

When they become despondent, an elegant lady presents herself and offers them the sum they need. They become uneasy because she is in the oldest profession on earth. They ask her to wait, and run off for advice.

"Rabbi, a woman wants to give us fifty thousand rubles to complete the synagogue."

"That's wonderful," says the rabbi.

"Yes, but this is a lady of easy virtue!"

"Oy vey!" cries the Rabbi. He thinks deeply, scratches his beard, nods his head, and says:

"You can take the money my friends. After all, we are only recycling."

✡ ✡ ✡

An ignorant social climber manages to bribe the shammes to rent a prestigious place by the eastern wall of the synagogue. The rabbi is surprised to see his new neighbor but says nothing. The social climber looks for a chance to exchange a few words, so during the part of the psalm "God saves people and animals" he asks:
"Rabbi, why did they group the animals with the people?"
"I blame the shammes."

✡ ✡ ✡

The rabbi of a small shtetl requires payments for every extra service he performs. A man asks him to give the funeral oration at his father's grave, and the rabbi outlines his proposals:
"I have a noble oration for 80 guldens, and a decent one for 50. And then there is one for 20 guldens which is very popular, but which I personally do not recommend."

✡ ✡ ✡

During a dreadful drought, the distraught people ask the rabbi to pray for rain. He prays, and rain begins to fall. It rains without respite for days, and water runs through the streets in torrents.
Everything sinks in the mud. The people now ask the rabbi to pray for sunshine. He prays for hours, but it rains harder than ever.
"You must understand," explains the rabbi's servant, "Our rabbi is still very young. He has just learnt how to start the rain but not yet how to switch it off."

✡ ✡ ✡

One day, in tsarist Russia, an old man asks the rabbi for help.

"They are taking my only son to the army! I don't have the gold to buy him out."

"Don't fret. I'll ask God to forbid the Tsar to recruit your only son."

The old man comes back after two weeks.

"Rabbi," he says bitterly, "They took my son after all."

"What can I do?" sighs the rabbi, "I can persuade God to give the order, but only He can make the Tsar obey."

✡ ✡ ✡

A buyer complains that his supplier is cheating him, which is a great sin against an honest man. The rabbi listens intently and says:

"You are right."

Soon after, the accused arrives and he in turn complains about the buyer. The rabbi listens to him and says:

"You are right."

The rabbi's wife who overheard both conversations is outraged: "How can you say such things? It's impossible for both to be right!"

"You are right."

✡ ✡ ✡

A marten's winter fur is very thick and valuable, but its summer coat is thin and worthless. A man comes to his rabbi to complain that his supplier sent him a dozen summer pelts instead of the winter ones that he had ordered.

"You are so impatient," says the rabbi. "Store them; It will be winter in no time."

✡ ✡ ✡

"How much do you earn"? asks the friend of a rabbi in a small kahal.

"Three guldens per week," replies the rabbi, and adds: "That's for a week in which they pay me at all."

In a steamy public bath a young man smacks the seat of someone he mistakes for his friend. He then notices that he has slapped the rabbi.

"Forgive me rabbi, I didn't know it was you."

"Don't worry," says the wise man. "I'm not a rabbi there!"

✧ ✧ ✧

The rabbi asks for a raise.

"How can a wise, god-fearing man be so greedy?" asks a representative of the community.

"So," replies the rabbi, "according to your logic, all the pleasures of this world are exclusively for fools and heathens?"

✧ ✧ ✧

When a community decides to dismiss its cantor, he asks for compensation of three hundred rubles. The people think this is too high, so they ask the rabbi for advice.

"Why ask me?" says the rabbi. "He knows how much it's worth to get rid of him"

✧ ✧ ✧

Someone tells the rabbi that Moshe was seen eating during a strict fast. When confronted with this, Moshe explains:

"Rabbi, I did it to help a poor girl get her dowry."

"What has her dowry to do with you breaking fast?"

"Well, when coming home from morning prayers, I heard a man say that he wished every Jewish girl as many thousands in her dowry as there will be Jews who will break this fast. And then I thought, why should I be the one to stop some poor girl from getting an extra thousand?"

✧ ✧ ✧

Someone tells the rabbi that Abram is trying to seduce Miriam, the innkeeper's wife.

The rabbi orders Abram to do penance. "This is a grave sin, you have to fast."

"But I'm much too ill to fast," pleads Abram.

"In that case you will pray for three hours each day."

"But rabbi, I have to earn for my family. Where will I find the time for prayer?"

"I see. Then you must give alms to the poor."

"But rabbi, with my earnings, I can barely feed my children!"

"You don't want to fast, or pray, or pay? So what do you want, you scoundrel?"

"I want Miriam!"

✡ ✡ ✡

A rich burgher drops in on a rabbi, who says that he is very honored by the visit.

"Think nothing of it," says the guest. "I was on my way to visit a Polish gentleman anyway."

Later, as the guest is leaving, the rabbi accompanies him to the door. "This is too great an honor" says the burgher.

"Think nothing of it," says the rabbi. "I was on my way to the outhouse anyway."

✡ ✡ ✡

A rabbi is worried. Donations for his synagogue are so small that there is never enough money. He reprimands his flock:

"You don't want to give donations, but you're just dying to be buried in a Jewish cemetery!"

✡ ✡ ✡

"Rabbi, where does rain come from?"

"You see, clouds are like sponges full of water. When the wind piles them up one against the other, it squeezes the water out."

"But what proof do we have that this happens?"

"Well, it's raining, isn't it?"

✡ ✡ ✡

A Jew had a chicken farm. One day, he runs to the rabbi.

"Half of my chickens are dead! What shall I do?"

"What do you feed them?"

"Barley."

"That's bad, give them wheat."

Within a week, half of the surviving chickens die. "Rabbi, it didn't help."

"And what do you give them to drink?"

"Cold water."

"That's bad, give them warm water."

After a few days, the Jew comes back with tears in his eyes,

"Rabbi, half of the remainder is gone."

"And where do you get the water?"

"From a well."

"That's bad. Get it from the spring."

After two days, the Jew comes weeping with despair.

"Rabbi nothing helped. I have only one little chicken left."

The rabbi sighs with compassion. "What a shame! I still have so much good advice to give you!"

✡ ✡ ✡

One day, before prayers, the rabbi notices that he has lost the key to the box in which he stored the torah. He turns to his congregation:

"Perhaps one of you has his pick-lock?" he asks.

Later, at prayer, he sees that his assistant has turned pale

"What is it?" he asks in a whisper.

"I just remembered that I forgot to lock the safe."

The rabbi glances at the congregation, and says:

"Don't worry; everyone's still present."

✡ ✡ ✡

The rabbi turns to the author of a commentary:

"You should write about Job rather than about Solomon."

"Do you think that I should explore the philosophical depths of the book of Job?"

"Not really. What I mean is that King Solomon was so exacting that I doubt if he would accept your commentary. But poor Job was crushed by so many misfortunes, that he would not notice another one."

✡ ✡ ✡

A rabbi says to an author:

"If you are going for a walk tonight, remember to take your book."

"Why?"

"Because it's written that evil spirits sometimes attack learned men at night. With your book you will be quite safe."

✡ ✡ ✡

A rabbi turns to a scholar of the Lamentations.

"I can respond to your interpretation of the Lamentations only with some of my own."

✡ ✡ ✡

The Chassidic rabbi had many visitors. He foretold their future and gave them advice. People often paid for this, which met with his servant's disapproval.

"But could you do what I'm doing?" asked the conceited rabbi.

"Only in part. I could give them advice and foretell their future, but to take their money with a straight face is beyond my talents."

✡ ✡ ✡

"Our rabbi can perform miracles."

"I don't believe it!"

"But I know a young man who was mentally ill. He went to our rabbi and came out cured."

"Ah, this I can believe. When he went it proves that he was disturbed, but when he left it proves that he came back to his senses."

✡ ✡ ✡

During a great drought there was a shortage of food. The orthodox rabbi told his faithful to fast, but the Chassidic rabbi told his flock to feast.

"We have to act so that those above can see that we really need food. If we fast, they may think that we can survive on nothing."

✡ ✡ ✡

A Chassid boasts that his rabbi prays day and night, and sleeps only one hour each day.

"Impossible, how can that be?"

"Simple, in that one hour he does more sleeping than others in a whole night."

✡ ✡ ✡

An Orthodox Jew is speaking to a Chassid:

"The miracles of rabbis are known only by hearsay, but I can tell you something I saw with my own eyes. A mother ran to our rabbi with tears in her eyes, told him that her child had died, and implored him to bring it back to life."

"Don't weep. I will pray and your child will live," he told her.

"And did it come back to life?" asked the Chassid.

"It didn't even stir."

"Well, where was the miracle?"

"Maybe there was no miracle, but I did see it with my own eyes."

✡ ✡ ✡

A non-believing Jew is weeping during prayers in the synagogue.

"What are you doing here if you don't believe in God?" asks a friend.

"There are two possibilities," the atheist replies. "If I'm wrong and God does exist, I'll get it in the neck for not believing. But if I'm right and God does not exist, then whom do I have to turn to?"

✡ ✡ ✡

On the last day of a holiday, the congregation prays for rain, which starts to fall immediately.

"You see, my prayers were answered at once," says the rabbi.

"Be careful," says a voice from the crowd. "Someone like you already caused the Deluge."

✡ ✡ ✡

A baker in a synagogue is shouting out his prayers at the top of his voice, and his neighbor whispers in his ear:

"You'll get His attention sooner if you make less noise, and bake bigger loaves."

✡ ✡ ✡

A cruise ship has sunk, and two Jewish friends are sitting in a rescue boat which is lost in the vastness of the ocean. There is nothing on the horizon. One of them is praying:

"Good Lord, if you save me, I'll donate half of my wealth to charity."

They float on into the night and no help arrives.

"Lord, if you save me, I'll give two thirds of my wealth to charity."

Morning comes, and their situation seems hopeless.

"Lord, if you save me from this trouble, I'll give three quarters of my wealth to charity."

At this point his friend cries: "Before you say another word, I see land!"

✡ ✡ ✡

A Jew is praying:

"Lord, let me win a lot of money on the lottery, and I swear that I will give half to the synagogue."

Unfortunately he wins nothing. He then tries a Christian church, lights a candle, and promises to give half his winnings to charity. To his delight, he wins two hundred zlotys.

"I must admit that the Christian God helped me more than ours," he thinks, "but ours is smarter. He knew that I didn't intend to donate that money in the first place!"

✡ ✡ ✡

2

In School

Religious learning was one of the keys for preserving Jewish culture in Poland. Children were taught from an early age in elementary schools (heders). More advanced studies were undertaken in Talmudic colleges (yeshivas).

✡ ✡ ✡

After a memorable sermon by a rabbi, one of the listeners throws a book on the table and says angrily:
"You stole the sermon word for word from this book!"
"What do you mean I stole it? It's still there, isn't it?"

✡ ✡ ✡

A listener weeps loudly during the sermon of a wandering preacher, who later goes up to him and asks:
"Did my sermon move you so deeply?"
"Not at all," replies the listener pausing in his sobs. "But I have a son who is training to be a preacher and I just realized what's in store for him."

✡ ✡ ✡

A melamed is trying to teach a very simple boy some basic knowledge, but the boy is exceptionally dull. The teacher decides to use a new technique.

"David, you will memorize five Hebrew words and you will imagine that they stand for the names of five of your neighbors."

"Yom- this will be Matthew, our blacksmith,"

"Hashish - that's old Ivan,"

"Vayehulu- that's Peter the locksmith,"

"Hashamayim- that's our forester,"

"Veharec- that's Igor."

David likes this idea and starts his prayers next day: "Yom Vayehulu..."

"You ass! You forgot about Hashish."

"No I didn't," says the boy proudly. "Old Hashish died last night."

✡ ✡ ✡

It is said about melameds that pupils are the first to hide from them. Later, when it comes to paying for the lessons, it is the parents who hide. And lastly, when the parents want to find out what their children have learned, it's the melameds who hide.

✡ ✡ ✡

"Why do they hire a melamed for only six months?"

"Because if he is honest he loses his nerve after six months with the children. If he survives six months, it proves that he is not putting his heart into his job and should be replaced at once."

✡ ✡ ✡

Melamed: "Which is faster, a pigeon or a horse?"

Pupil: "If on foot, the horse."

✡ ✡ ✡

A melamed is trying to explain the might of God to little Moriz. He searches for a suitable example to illustrate the wonder of the things which He created.

"Just look how beautifully the Lord has covered this pond with ice."
"It's winter! What else should cover it?" replies Moriz.

✡ ✡ ✡

Melamed: "Rebecca, repeat what I have taught you about Moses."
Rebecca: "Moses was the son of an Egyptian princess."
"But Rebecca, you did not understand, the princess only found him in a basket."
"That's your opinion."

✡ ✡ ✡

A melamed asks the children: "Why did God create cats?" Nobody knows.
"To hunt mice. And why did he create dogs?"
This time the children know the answer: "To guard homes."
"And sheep?"
Nobody answers, and the melamed prompts:
"Well Moriz, what is your vest made out of?"
"My dad's old pants."

✡ ✡ ✡

A melamed becomes dependent on alcohol and loses his job. His friends are trying to persuade him to stop drinking, so that they could hire him again.
"Some logic!" he replies. "I taught so that I could drink, and now I have to give up drink so that I can teach!"

✡ ✡ ✡

A grandfather is watching his grandson do his lessons.

"All my life I marveled that left-handed people wrote so neatly."

"But I'm not left handed."

"So I see."

✫ ✫ ✫

"Imagine, rich Mandelstam has earned one hundred thousand rubles last year."

"Bah," says a poor melamed. "If I worked eight hundred school seasons I would also earn one hundred thousand rubles."

✫ ✫ ✫

Two students wonder whether God exists. Their discussion lasts several hours, and they agree that there is no God. One of them then brings some water to drink, and starts to intone a blessing.

"What are you doing? Didn't we just agree that there is no God?"

"Whether God exists or not, since when does a Jew drink water without a blessing?"

✫ ✫ ✫

A student falls asleep while studying in a yeshiva. When he wakes he sees that the room is empty, and that his yarmulke is missing.

"Where can it be?" he muses looking around.

He notices that some other yarmulke is lying on the seat beside him, and reasons:

"Is it my colleague's or is it mine? If it is his, where is mine? If it is mine, why is it on his seat? Did it fall off when I was sleeping, or did he play a joke and lift it from my head? Why should I worry about his yarmulke? Is he worried about mine? I bet he isn't. I'll just take his."

✫ ✫ ✫

Looking through the window of a yeshiva, someone notices that the students are smoking cigarettes on the Sabbath. All three are summoned before the rabbi.

"What were you thinking of?" he asks the first one.

"Forgive me rabbi; I forgot this was the Sabbath."

"And you?" he asks the second one.

"I forgot there is no smoking on the Sabbath."

"And I forgot to draw the curtains," says the third.

✡ ✡ ✡

Two yeshiva students are strolling through a town in falling snow. One of them says dreamily: "I wish that every snow flake was a golden gulden. God, how rich and happy I would be!"

"And how much of that money would you give me?" asks his friend.

"Not a cent!"

'That's awful! I didn't expect that from you."

"Why should I give you my money? Make your own wish."

✡ ✡ ✡

A student is reading late into the night. Suddenly, he hears a strange noise, and begins to reason as he was taught:

"If it's a cat, let it prowl, it won't harm me and it may catch a mouse. If this is a ghost, then I will pray and be quite safe, but if it's a thief? Heeeeelp!!"

✡ ✡ ✡

Two poor students were invited for breakfast by a rich man. Afterwards, the cook wrapped some sausage for them for the next day.

That night, one of them wakes up hungry and starts to look for the sausage. He goes through his friend's pockets but finds nothing. The sausage had disappeared. Next morning he challenges his friend:

"How could you? You ate the whole sausage yourself!"

"Not at all! I hid it in your pocket, the only place that you would not search if you woke up hungry during the night"

✡ ✡ ✡

Shalom is laboring over thick books in Hebrew. "The righteous sins seven times each day," he reads. Astonished, he holds his head:

"Impossible he must be boasting!"

✡ ✡ ✡

Why did Moses get two tablets from God on Mount Sinai? After he climbed the mountain, God asked him:

"Moses, do you want me to give you a tablet with my commandments?"

"How much does it cost?"

"It costs nothing."

"Then give me two."

✡ ✡ ✡

One day Daniel was reading about the golden calf.

"I don't understand," he muses, "Why the Jews, who were such a large nation, gave so little money. They could afford a great bull instead of a little calf."

"Don't you understand?" asks his friend. "They didn't bring their entire gold straight to Aaron. It was gathered by tax collectors. So, it's a miracle that enough of it survived to make a golden flea, never mind a calf!"

✡ ✡ ✡

People called Solomon wise because he reconciled two mothers who had a dispute over a child.

"Big deal," thinks Izzy. "If he could name the father, that would be something!"

✡ ✡ ✡

"Moriz, did you already study the ten commandments?"
"No uncle, we are still stuck on the ten plagues."

✡ ✡ ✡

The melamed is reading the bible in Hebrew with little David, and is translating individual words:

"Vatamot means 'she died,' Sarah means Sarah. So David, who was it that died?"

"Vatamot died" the child replies

"Don't you understand anything? Vatamot in Polish means 'she died,' and Sarah means Sarah. So who died?"

"In-Polish died."

"You ass! Vatamot means she died. Sarah died! So who died?"

Little David panics: "First Vatamot died, then in-Polish died, and now even Sarah died! Is this an epidemic?"

✡ ✡ ✡

A Jew reads in his prayer book: 'And you chose us from amongst all the nations.'

"Lord of the universe!" he cries. "Now what?"

✡ ✡ ✡

3

In A Small Town

"Do you know, Rebecca, they say that the Messiah will come soon. I am not at all happy about this, because we'd have to leave everything and go to Israel. And where will we be able to buy such a beautiful house as we have here?"

"Don't worry Moshe, God saved us from the Pharaoh, he will save us from the Messiah."

✡ ✡ ✡

A Jew from Kasrylevka must flee to Palestine. He looks at the house he has to leave behind and thinks:

"Dear lord, we prayed for two thousand years to go back to Jerusalem, and it had to happen to me!"

✡ ✡ ✡

Old Shalom is sitting on the porch thinking. A group of children gathers round expecting to hear a story. The old man sighs and says:

"In this world, our life is much harder than that of goys. But in the other world we will have a better life than they."

After a long silence he adds:

"There will be a riot if we don't!"

✡ ✡ ✡

The cobbler Mendel is deep in thought:
"God created this world very badly" he complains.
"You mean that you'd do a better job?" asks his foreman.
"Well, I would definitely make some things better than He."
"For example?"
"Shoes."

✡ ✡ ✡

"Chaim," says a delighted friend, "I saw you praying fervently in the synagogue today, and yet you said that you do not believe in God."
"That's true, but how can I be sure that I'm right?"

After a funeral, a Chassidic Jew is dancing and singing joyfully: "You came from dust and will turn into dust."

A neighbor sees him and asks: "Why are you dancing? Isn't this a sad occasion?" "Why sad?" replies the Jew. "If man was created from gold and turned to dust it would be sad, but if he starts as dust, and ends as dust, and has some vodka in between, why shouldn't he make merry?"

✯ ✯ ✯

A client comes to a watchmaker with a claim.

"My watch stopped to-day, and you swore that it would go for the rest of my life!"

"Don't shout. Is it my fault that last month you looked like a corpse? You should thank God that you're feeling better."

✯ ✯ ✯

Two neighbors are talking:
    Kowalski: "My son passed his entrance exam to high school."
    Rosenblum: "Why does he need high school?"
    Kowalski: "He will be able to become a priest, and later a bishop or even a Cardinal."
    Rosenblum: "So?"
    Kowalski: "And maybe even a pope! I don't understand why you are not impressed. What do you expect, that he becomes God?"
    "One of ours did."

✯ ✯ ✯

A Jew tells his innkeeper that the vodka brew he makes is wonderful.

"How do you manage it?" he asks.

"Very simple," the innkeeper says. "I take rye vodka, I add herbs and honey, and let it soak for eight days in a cool room."

"That's not what I mean. How do you manage not to drink it before the eight days are up?"

✯ ✯ ✯

A shammes dies during a long drought. The citizens put a prayer for rain into his coffin, a prayer that he is to take to the Almighty. Someone whispers:

"Lord, hurry and grant this wish, which we send through our shammes, because if you don't, you'll soon have our whole kahal on your hands."

✡ ✡ ✡

A Jewish woman passing by a railway station sees a Jew smoking a cigarette.

"Shame on you! May I have a stroke and drop dead! A Jew, sitting in a railway station and smoking on the Sabbath!"

The smoker replies calmly: "Get ready for ten strokes. another nine Jews are smoking in the waiting room."

✡ ✡ ✡

An old Jew turns to a young man: "You should be ashamed of your sin! How can you eat during such a holy day? Look at me, I am old and ill and yet I keep my fast."

The young man nods and replies sadly: "Neither of us will go to heaven. I because I do not keep my fast, and you because there is no heaven in the first place."

✡ ✡ ✡

A Jew from Mazepovka is visiting Warsaw. His son is showing him around. Suddenly, the old man stops in the middle of the road and starts to scratch himself.

"Father, don't do this here, this is not your village."

"So, every time I get an itch I have to go to Mazepovka?"

✡ ✡ ✡

An informer dies in a small town. Nobody can remember anything good about the man, anything that could be used during the funeral prayers. Suddenly, someone has an idea.

"We can say this good thing about him, that he has left behind him two sons, compared with whom he was pure gold!"

✶ ✶ ✶

"Where are you rushing to Moriz?"
"I tell you, in that cinema, there is a film with a beautiful woman. In the third part of the film she stops at a stream and starts to undress, but a train passes by and hides everything. The third part is about to start."
"So why are you in such a hurry?"
"I thought that if this is a Polish train it may be late."

✶ ✶ ✶

"Did you know that old Eierveiss has died? Are you going to his funeral?"
"Why should I go to his funeral? Will he come to mine?"

✶ ✶ ✶

Its evening and Itzhak is running home. A friend stops him:
"Where are you running from?"
"The theater."
"And what's the show?"
"Omelet."
"Omelet?"
"No, wait a minute, Hamlet. I liked it very much"
"So why are you running?"
"Because someone shouted 'a hit, a hit!' And who always gets hit first? The Jews! I'm taking no chances!"

✶ ✶ ✶

Old Abe buys a ticket to the baths and is surprised that such a small puddle costs two zlotys. He is advised to buy a long term ticket for twelve baths at a discount rate.

"Twelve baths? And who will guarantee that I will live so long?"

✡ ✡ ✡

Two Jews are sitting in a cafe, watching passers-by
"Do you see who David is walking with?"
"Why shouldn't I see?"
"She's a fine woman. He lives with her."
"What a nasty thing to say. He lived with her once and the whole of Warsaw says that he lives with her."
They meet again next day.
"Do you know that Solomon's wife is fooling around with Leisman?"
"What gossip is that?"
"They were seen together in a forest."
"Oy vey, three trees and they call it a forest!"
On the third day the talkative friend is silent.
"What is it, why don't you speak?"
After a long pause, his friend clears his throat and says: "They say that I am sleeping with your Sarah."
"Thank God! I thought you lost your voice!"

✡ ✡ ✡

Each Sabbath, an old cantor comes to borrow one hundred rubles from a banker. The banker lends the money without question because the old man always pays it back. One day, his curiosity gets the better of him and he asks:

"Tell me, why do you need this money which you borrow each Friday and give back each Monday? You don't even spend it because you return the same bank notes I gave you."

"That's true. I do not spend it because I would have nothing to repay it from later on. But when I feel those rubles in my pocket, I sing like a bird!"

✡ ✡ ✡

Moses knocks on Yankel's window late in the evening.
"Yankel, are you asleep?"
"Not yet."
"Then lend me fifty guldens"
"Go away; can't you see that I'm sleeping?"

✡ ✡ ✡

Hello Chaim!" shouts a Jew on a street and slaps a passer-by on his shoulder.
The startled passer-by turns in alarm.
"Oy vey! Where do you know me from? I can't quite place you. Did we launch one of those speculative little companies that go bust in the night? Was it the warehouse that caught fire? Maybe in a cell when I was falsely accused of forgery? Or was it at a bar-mitzvah which I gate-crashed? And besides, my name's not Chaim."

✡ ✡ ✡

Two shopkeepers meet. "How's business?"
"Very bad. I am losing money nearly every day."
"Then how do you live?"
"I close my shop at week-ends, and then I don't lose money. I live on that."

✡ ✡ ✡

Moses says to his wife: "From to-day, I don't want to have anything to do with that Apfelbaum."

"Why not"?

"Because people say that his daughter is running around with boys."

"But Moses, he doesn't even have a daughter!"

"What's the difference? I still don't want to have anything to do with someone whose daughter, if he had one, would run around with boys."

☆ ☆ ☆

A woman is leading a goat she bought at the market. A neighbor asks her:

"What do you want with a goat?"

"My husband fell ill, and the doctor prescribed goat milk every day."

"And do you have room in the barn?"

"No, it will have to live in our house."

"But what about the smell?"

"Nu, it'll just have to get used to it."

☆ ☆ ☆

4

If I Were As Rich As Rothschild

A poor village tailor is asked what he would do if he were as rich as Rothschild.

"Ask rather what would Rothschild do if he was a pauper like I am. But if I were as rich as Rothschild, I would stop haggling with customers who try to lower the price. I would price my garments at least at two guldens, take it or leave it!"

✫ ✫ ✫

Baron Rothschild is going home in a taxi. The meter shows $40.00 and the baron pays $50.00. The driver is not very impressed.

"Your son is more generous."

"He can afford to be. He has a rich father, while I have a spendthrift son."

✫ ✫ ✫

Rothschild helped two poor brothers with monthly donations of 200 guldens. When one of them dies, the other one, wearing a black arm band, comes for his usual payment. The baron murmurs his condolences and pays him 200 guldens. The poor man takes them, but does not make any motion to leave.

"Where is my brother's portion?"

"But you just told me that he died."

"Is that a reason for you to grow rich on my inheritance?"

✫ ✫ ✫

Baron Rothschild says to his clerk:

"Mr. Silverman, this will not do. You start work at ten o'clock and even then you are late. Look at me, I'm the boss after all, yet I come punctually at eight."

"It's easy for you to come at eight," replies the clerk, "that's what makes you Baron Rothschild. But for a humble clerk like me even ten o'clock is far too early."

✫ ✫ ✫

Ignaz gets a measure of cloth and asks a tailor to make him a suit. The tailor measures the material very carefully, and says that there is too little cloth for a suit. Ignaz takes the cloth to another tailor, who is delighted to oblige. On the Sabbath, Ignaz wears his new suit, and sees that his tailor has a small son whose trousers are from the same material.

He later goes back to the first tailor and says: "Your measuring was wrong. Another tailor made me a suit, and still had enough material to clothe his little son. Why could you not do it?"

"Because I have twins."

✫ ✫ ✫

A peanut vendor sets up his wheel cart in front of Rothschild's bank. One day, a friend asks him for a loan. The vendor replies sadly:

"I could have done it last week but not today. I agreed with Rothschild that he won't sell peanuts if I don't lend money."

✫ ✫ ✫

A beggar passing by Rothschild's villa sees his little son wheeled out for a walk in the park. He thinks a while, shakes his head, sighs and mutters:

"So young, and already a Rothschild."

✫ ✫ ✫

A reporter asks a millionaire at an interview how he made his fortune.

"I started with nothing," the rich man says. "As a child, I roamed the streets and lived from what people gave me. One day, I found two groshes and bought some peanuts. I sold those peanuts for four groshes and bought two bags which I later sold for eight groshes. Things started to look up. In time I managed to earn two zlotys for which I bought a brush and some boot polish. After two years as a shoe shine, I managed to save 15 zlotys. I bought a new suit and became a porter. And just around that time my aunt in New York died and left me nine hundred thousand dollars."

✫ ✫ ✫

A banker was bankrupted and disgraced by his forgeries of bills and documents. He now tries a new career as a writer. One of the literary critics of his first book observes:

"His writing is poetic justice. Papers wasted him, and now he's wasting paper."

✫ ✫ ✫

Representatives of a kahal approach the local banker to help them build a new fence around their ancient cemetery.

"It's not worth spending a single kopeck for a fence," replies the rich man. "Why put anything around the cemetery? The living are not jostling to get in, and the residents are not likely to walk out."

✫ ✫ ✫

A Jew manages to save twenty thousand rubles, but has no head for business. He asks his banker for advice about where to invest his money, and the risks involved. The rich man replies:

"It all depends on what you value more in life, good food or good sleep."

✫ ✫ ✫

"Please give me something, even a few kopeks will help," asks a beggar. "After all, we both come from the same town."

"That's impossible, because you'd know that I never give anything to anyone.

✯ ✯ ✯

A poor man asks a millionaire: "Tell me, how can I get rich?"

"Start by being a mean, stingy, heartless penny pincher for the first twenty years."

"And afterwards?"

"Afterwards? Afterwards you'll stay like that for the rest of your life."

✯ ✯ ✯

"Do you know Solomon Greenberg? He is very rich. When he lived here twenty years ago, he had only one pair of threadbare trousers, and now he has millions."

"So? What good will millions of pairs of threadbare trousers do him?"

✯ ✯ ✯

"Since my fortunes have improved, guests are swarming into my house through doors and windows. I can't stand it any longer!"

"There's a simple remedy for this: ask the rich ones for large loans, and give some small loans to the poor ones. You will never see either again."

✯ ✯ ✯

A poor man turns to his stingy relative: "My daughter is becoming an old maid. Help me to get her married. Give me 500 guldens for a dowry."

"I can't manage that right now, business is bad; but if your daughter comes to my accountant on the first of each month, he will pay her 10 guldens. After all we are related. I swear that I'll keep helping her as long as I live."

"Knowing how mean you are, you're liable to die tomorrow!"

✡ ✡ ✡

A rich man who can't write is using a poor melamed to write his letters for nothing. The poor man's friend cannot understand this:

"You fool! Why do you write his letters if he doesn't pay you?"

"And you think he would pay me if I didn't write?"

✡ ✡ ✡

A beggar says to his colleague: "Oy-vey! I completely forgot to-day to beg from Rothschild. He always gives me a gulden."

"What a shame, you'll just have to let him off this time."

"A generous man like that, why should I let him off?"

✡ ✡ ✡

5

Rich Men And Paupers

A beggar asks a passer-by for help.
  "Bah! So young, so healthy! Can't you use your strength for something better than begging?"
  "So! Trying to weasel out of charity?" the beggar demands, rolling up his sleeves. "I'll show you in a minute how I can use my youth and strength!"

✻ ✻ ✻

A beggar turns to a rich man: "Since your coffers are so full, and mine are so terribly depleted, I turn to you with a respectful plea to take account of my distressing poverty, and to perform the noble and praiseworthy task of giving me some charity."
  "Listen!" the annoyed man says. "Why do you put on such airs when you ask for money?"
  "Oh? Are you trying to teach me my trade?"

✻ ✻ ✻

A beggar who was invited to a rich man's table shows a child-like delight at the sight of a beautiful vase.

"Why are you so happy?" asks the rich man. "After all, this vase belongs to me."

"What's the difference? We both get the same pleasure when we look at it."

"Yes, but I can throw it out or destroy it, and you can't."

"Then neither of us will have that pleasure."

"True, but I can also give it away or sell it."

"Then you'll be the only loser."

✡ ✡ ✡

A beggar comes to a rich merchant and asks for charity. The merchant asks him to take a seat and wait. An hour passes, and then another, but the merchant is still bent over his books. Finally, the beggar gets up to leave.

"Be patient," the merchant asks politely. "I will know in a few minutes whether I can give you something, or whether I'll have to join you."

✡ ✡ ✡

A rich man becomes ill, and is handing out generous gifts of charity all around. "He is not as mean as he used to be before his illness," remarks a beggar.

"That's because the money he is giving so freely now belongs to his heirs."

✡ ✡ ✡

The rabbi of a very poor kahal makes his rounds of neighboring villages asking for funds. The rabbi's assistant shows up shortly afterwards.

"But your rabbi was already here a minute ago," says the farmer.

"Are you surprised? If our cantor had shoes, he'd also pay you a visit."

✡ ✡ ✡

A beggar approaches a rich factory manager. "I am asking for charity. I'm a poor musician and a father of five."

The rich man gives him some money and says: "If I remember, you were a poor artisan last week."

"In these hard times one profession is not enough."

✧ ✧ ✧

"My cousin in Munich is very poor. If he was not in the habit of fasting all day twice a week he would have died of hunger long ago."

✧ ✧ ✧

A rich man invites two beggars to a wedding. They admire the interior of his house, the fittings and antique furniture. As they leave after the feast one says to the other:

"Do you know, I'd gladly give my shirt to be as rich as he."

✧ ✧ ✧

A pauper asks his doctor to give him something for his appetite.

"You look healthy, but I'll examine you to find out why you've lost your appetite."

"You don't understand. My appetite is far greater than my income. That's why I need something for it."

✧ ✧ ✧

6

Jokers

Hershel from Ostropol and Motke from Vilna were real people who passed into legend. Their humor was mocking, irreverent and defiant, the humor of survivors who strive to live fully in spite of poverty and social pressures.

✡ ✡ ✡

"Hershel, I hear that you don't believe in God."
"Who says so?"
"People."
"Don't listen to people. Ask Him instead!"

✡ ✡ ✡

Hershel was a notorious liar. The rabbi had enough of it.
"Stop it! If you can open your mouth without lying I'll give you a ruble."
"A ruble? But we agreed on two!"

✡ ✡ ✡

The rabbi had another serious problem with Hershel, who loved to drink not only on the Sabbath but every day of the year. What was worse, he drank vodka and spirits with the same abandon as he drank wine. It was the rabbi's duty to reprimand him.
"Hershel, why do you drink?"
"To drown my sorrows."

"And haven't you drowned them yet?"
"They've just learned how to swim."

✡ ✡ ✡

Hershel found a small apartment for his family in Ostropol, but soon, the owner was going crazy trying to get him to pay the rent, and finally decided to evict him. Hershel tried to convince him not to do this:

"You're making a big mistake. I tell you this for your own good. You won't know the new tenant, and what will happen? You won't be able to sleep at night. You'll be tormented by doubt whether he will or will not pay, but with me you'll have peace of mind because you can be sure that I won't pay."

✡ ✡ ✡

Hershel takes every opportunity to earn extra money, and he sometimes hires himself out as a marriage broker. One day, he knocks on the door of a rich, proud man who has a daughter of marriageable age.

"I have found a great partner for your daughter."

"Thank God, and who is the candidate?"

"Abel, the cobbler's son."

"What? That good-for-nothing loafer, drunk and scoundrel? For my daughter? Are you making fun of me?"

The rich man then grabs Herschel by the collar and throws him out. Three days later Herschel comes back.

"I found another partner, this time a serious one. It is Burl, the rabbi's son."

Splendid, I accept. And did you talk with the rabbi? Does he agree?"

"I've just seen him. When I suggested your daughter, he said 'what? My son for the daughter of that ignorant oaf? Are you making fun of me?' And then he grabbed me by the collar and threw me out!"

✡ ✡ ✡

A joker wrote to the rabbi of Ostropol: "Rabbi, if you are so clever, please answer these questions: How big is my estate? How much am I worth? How heavy is the moon? and, what am I thinking of at this moment?"

The rabbi thought this was a stupid joke, but Hershel offered to reply for him. He wrote: "First, measure the length and width of your field, and I will tell you the size of your estate. Second, you are worth as much as Abraham who compared himself to a grain of sand. Third, the moon weighs two pounds, and if you don't believe this weigh it yourself. Fourth, at this moment you're thinking that our rabbi is answering your stupid questions. but it's I, Hershel."

✡ ✡ ✡

Justice triumphs in the end. At last Herschel meets someone smarter than himself. One day, he is sitting on the wall of a field owned by a rich merchant. He scratches himself with both hands over his whole body, grunting with contentment. The rich man comes out and asks what he's doing.

"It's so good to scratch an itch. I haven't bathed or eaten for three weeks." Touched by this, the rich man invites him inside. Hershel baths for a long time, then sits down to a huge meal, eats his fill, and stuffs his pockets with sweets.

Next day, the rich man sees Hershel in exactly the same spot, but in the company of another beggar. Both are scratching themselves and grunting with pleasure.

"Hey you two dirty vagabonds stop scratching and get out!"

"What's happened? You helped me yesterday, but now you're throwing me out!"

"I helped you yesterday because you were alone. There are two of you to-day. Go and scratch each other."

✡ ✡ ✡

One day, Hershel stops in front of the grave of a rich family from Ostropol. He contemplates it for a long time. His eye lingers on the golden letters, the trimmed grass, the splendid bouquets, and he sighs: "That's what I call living."

✡ ✡ ✡

So many people called Hershel an ass that he liked to tell stories about animals. His favorite story went like this:

"The head and the tail of a serpent spent many years crawling in the dust of the roads. One day, the tail said to the head: 'Enough of this. I am always in the rear and you always pull me wherever you want. Let's change places.'

The head thought about this, and agreed. But the tail couldn't see, or hear, or smell anything. Soon, they were trampled by passers-by, and soiled by the waste of farm animals. Then the tail felt a cart approaching, and, trying to get out of its way, fell into a ditch full of nettles and thorns."

"Who's responsible? Those who lead must be able to see where they're going. The tail can't lead, because it has no eyes, so it can't be blamed. But the head agreed to be led by the blind, so the head is to blame."

✡ ✡ ✡

Herschel is daydreaming.

"I would like my house to burn down tonight, so that I could jump out of the window wearing only the shirt on my back."

"Since when does anyone wish for such things?" asks a friend. "It would be a terrible misfortune!"

"Why a misfortune?" Herschel demands, surprised. "At last I'd have a shirt."

✡ ✡ ✡

A rich man challenges Motke: "Is it true what people say, that you've become a revolutionary? That you're protesting against the order of our world that divides people into the rich and the poor?"

"But sir," Mote replies, "I don't object that some should be rich and others poor, only that I am one of the others!"

✡ ✡ ✡

Motke is musing about the local rich man:
"He never gives to charity in the summer because it's too hot to put his hand in his pocket, nor in the winter because it is too cold to pull it out."

✡ ✡ ✡

Motke is weeping after the death of his wife, and the rabbi tries to console him:
"But Motke, don't you believe in the resurrection and eternal life thereafter?"
"Yes rabbi, that's why I'm weeping."

✡ ✡ ✡

Since no one pays much attention to him, Motke complains:
"You look on me with contempt, yet I know for a fact that countess Rudnicka is prepared to pay one thousand rubles just to see me."
His words make a big impression.
"One thousand rubles you say? Just to see you?"
"Yes, the poor lady is blind."

7

The Wise Men Of Chelm

According to a legend, the angel who was scattering foolish people among the nations ripped the bag that held them, and they all fell into Chelm. Chelm is a real town near Lublin, built on a steep hill by a river. The drinking water was very bad, so people took it from the river. The act of carrying empty pails downhill and full pails uphill may have started the legend (Horacy Safrin).

✧ ✧ ✧

A man stops a passer-by in Chelm. "Could you please tell me the time?"
 The passer-by takes out a large, ornate gold watch from the pocket of his vest, and says:
 "It will be four o'clock in ten minutes."
 "I didn't ask you what time it will be in ten minutes. What is it now?"

✧ ✧ ✧

A Jew from Chelm. is writing to his uncle, and is using very large letters.
 "Why do you write with such large letters?" asks his friend.
 "So that my uncle can understand more easily. He is a bit deaf you know."

✧ ✧ ✧

A peasant brings a cow to the market in Chelm. It is old and emaciated, it eats a great deal of hay, and no longer gives milk. The peasant wants to sell it, but no one is in any hurry to buy it.

Suddenly, Yankel arrives on the scene and offers his services to sell the cow. He assumes a theatrical pose, and intones:

"I invite all connoisseurs of fine cattle to look at this prize exhibit, even though the less informed are not able to recognize its virtues! What can one say about this cow? At first glance it's not impressive, but take a closer look. This is the most sensational beast in the district. It eats like a sparrow, and gives twenty liters of milk each day. It is so strong that it can pull a plow like an ox. Its calves are the fattest in the neighborhood. Who among you, my friends, wouldn't want to own such a miraculous animal?"

A group forms around them. Some ask the price, which Yankel raises continually. At this point, the peasant pulls on his sleeve and whispers:

"If this cow is as good as you say, I'd rather keep it myself"

✯ ✯ ✯

A man from Chelm goes into a hat shop and begins to turn out his pockets.

"What are you looking for?" the sales assistant asks him.

"I would like to buy a hat, and I had the size of my head written on a card, but I think I forgot it at home."

"The card or the head?"

"What card and what head?"

"Which did you leave at home?"

"Why would I leave my head at home?"

"If you took your card…"

"But I did not take my card."

"But you wanted to take it. Why do you need a card if you have your head?"

"I'm not sure. My wife often tells me that I run around as if I lost my head."

"So you've lost both your card and your head?"

"Stop! All your stupid questions are making my head spin!"

"Fine, then you must have your head, for how could it spin if you didn't have it? Let's measure it for a hat."

✯ ✯ ✯

Rosenzweig was very absent-minded. One day, when staying overnight in a hotel, he made a detailed list of where to find everything when he woke up next morning. He ended the list with: "And I myself am in bed."

Next morning, he found and ticked off everything on the list, but when he looked at the bed, he noted with horror that he was not in it!

"I mustn't panic," he thought.

"It's most unlikely that I was abducted by a gang, because Ostropol is such a quiet town. No, it's more likely that I simply fell off my bed."

As he was getting down on his knees to look under the bed, he caught a glimpse of himself in the mirror.

"Here I am!" he beamed with relief.

✭ ✭ ✭

A young man from Chelm complains to his father that he is hungry.

"We have nothing in the pantry to-day," sighs the father, "but I have an idea. We have a good neighbor who always has food, but you shouldn't just beg for it. If you go to him in a long robe with an air of mystery, however, and ask him to guess what you are, he will guess that you are a horse or a camel, and you will reply that he did not guess right, and that you are hungry. He's sure to laugh, and to feed you."

The young man does as his father suggests, and knocks on his neighbor's door.

"Guess who I am?" he asks.

"An ass!"

"Wrong!" the happy youth cries out."I'm a horse or a camel. Now feed me!"

✭ ✭ ✭

A fire starts in Chelm. and everyone runs to put it out. A voice is heard from the crowd:

"How lucky that the fire was right here. Otherwise it would be so dark that we wouldn't see anything, and we wouldn't be able to find it."

✭ ✭ ✭

The shammes in Chelm had aged a great deal. He found it very difficult to go from house to house, and knock on doors to rouse his congregation for morning prayers.

The good people of Chelm, touched with compassion for their beloved shammes, met to discuss the best way to ease his burden. One day, he woke to find all the doors of his flock stacked neatly in his courtyard, so that he could knock on them without having to walk.

✡ ✡ ✡

A man drowned in the local pond. A woman, whose husband disappeared the previous month, thinks he may have drowned. She goes to the rabbi for a death certificate.

The rabbi asks: "How do you know that this naked, disfigured man is your husband? Can you recall any special feature which would identify him?"

After a short while the woman replies: "Yes rabbi, he stuttered."

The rabbi ponders this. "That's not enough; in Chelm many people stutter."

✡ ✡ ✡

In a house in Chelm, a dog has climbed on the table and is licking the ladle. The servant just sits there without reacting. The man of the house looks into the kitchen and says angrily:

"Why don't you chase that dog away?"

"I can't. It tore my trousers yesterday and we're not on speaking terms."

✡ ✡ ✡

The man of the house told his servant to wake him up at five. The servant wakes him at three and says:

"I just wanted to tell you, you can sleep for another two hours before I wake you."

✡ ✡ ✡

David reads in a book that men with thick beards can be really stupid. He is very upset because his own beard is as thick as a birch broom. But then he thinks:

"The Torah clearly forbids the pious to shave their beards, but nowhere is it forbidden to burn them."

He then takes out a match and sets his beard on fire, painfully burning his face. Angry, he takes a pen and, beside the sentence which spoke of the folly of thick bearded men, he adds a margin note: "Tested and confirmed."

✡ ✡ ✡

Dialogue in a Chelm Post office:
"When does the post leave for Pinsk?"
"Every day."
"Including Monday?"
"Yes."
"And on Tuesday?"
"Also."
"And on Wednesday?"
"Also."
"Then why didn't you say so at once?"

✡ ✡ ✡

A woman is buying bread and herrings in the market:
"How much?"
"Fourteen."
"Why fourteen? I thought it was eleven."
"The herrings cost seven, the bread also seven, fourteen altogether."
"I don't know what system you use, but it is clearly eleven. I have four children from my first marriage, and my husband also has four children from his first marriage, and later we had three of our own. So each of us has seven, and we have eleven in all."

✡ ✡ ✡

A man in Chelm turns to a young boy: "You pass an elderly person in the street without taking off your cap? What sort of up-bringing is that?"

"This is my brother's cap, and his manners are terrible!"

✡ ✡ ✡

A visitor asks a man from Chelm: "Why are there three clocks on the tower of your main square?"

"Don't you see? Whenever someone looks at the clock to see the time, other people have additional faces to look at without having to wait their turn."

✡ ✡ ✡

"Please explain to me," says Moshe to his friend: "Why does the sun shine in the summer when it is warm and nobody needs it, and disappears in the winter when we have frosts and snow?"

His friend, also a deep thinker, replies: "I have been pondering a question which is even more profound. Why does the sun shine during the day when it is light, and hides at night when darkness falls, leaving the poor little moon to do all the work by itself?"

✡ ✡ ✡

A rabbi traveling by cart up a hill sees workers laying asphalt. He asks the driver what they are doing.

"It will be easier to climb the hill on asphalt" says the driver.

"I understand why they are doing it uphill," says the rabbi after they top the crest, "but what's the point of doing it downhill?"

8

How People Talk

A man, at a loss as to where to spend his vacations, arrives at his friend's house. He is greeted warmly, since his friends expect him to stay only a few days. A week passes, then a second, and the guest gives no hint that he wants to leave. His friends decide to get rid of him delicately, and devise a plan:

"To-morrow, at lunch, we will start a senseless quarrel. He'll get mixed up in it, taking my side or yours and that'll be the perfect excuse to throw him out."

The next day, the couple starts an argument, raising their voices and using the most blood-curdling insults. The guest, however, keeps eating in silence. Finally, the exasperated host asks:

"How can you sit there in silence when this witch insults me like that?"

"Since I still have to stay here for another five weeks," their guest replies, "It will be better if I don't get mixed up in your private quarrels."

✼ ✼ ✼

"Imagine, Yankel got lost in a snow storm. He had frostbite on both hands by the time they found him."

"Mercy, what will he talk with now?"

✼ ✼ ✼

"Why are you so quiet to-day?"

"In such a cold I should take the hands out of my pockets?"

✼ ✼ ✼

"Moshe, your signet ring is beautiful! But why do you wear it with the diamond inside, towards the palm?"

"What a stupid question! Do we talk palms up or palms down?"

✼ ✼ ✼

A Jew passing a cemetery hears the most frightful moans. He sees a man on his knees, lamenting by a grave: "How could you do this to me?'

"You unfortunate man," the passer-by says compassionately. "You must have lost someone very close to you."

"Do you know," says the man lifting his tear-stained face, "I never even met him. He was my wife's first husband. How could he die so young?"

✼ ✼ ✼

"Moshe, I've just learned about a very gifted apothecary who can transform iron into gold. All you have to do is to heat the iron and sprinkle it with a special powder that he can sell you. The only condition is that you must not think of polar bears at any time during that process."

"Oy! Give me his name at once!"

A few days later, the friends meet again, and Moshe cries out angrily:

"Devil take that apothecary! I never even knew that polar bears existed until you told me. But yesterday, when I was making gold, whole legions of them danced around me wherever I looked."

✡ ✡ ✡

An aged woman muses: "People say that our youth to-day have worse manners now than in the old days, but I think that the opposite is true. I remember how I couldn't cross the street fifty years ago without being whistled at, but now all the boys treat me with respect."

✡ ✡ ✡

A letter came when you were out, saying that your father is dead," says the wife.

"I don't believe a word of it. This is not my father's writing."

✡ ✡ ✡

A client enters a shop. "I'd like a powder for fleas."

"What amount?"

"How should I know? Millions!"

✡ ✡ ✡

"Mister Apfelkreuz, what happened to that beautiful walking stick you had, the one with the ivory griffin handle?"

"I'm walking with it now."

"But where's the griffin?"

"I had to cut it off; the stick became too long for me."

"Then why didn't you shorten it at the bottom?"

"Because its length there was just right."

✯ ✯ ✯

Two friends are having a discussion:

"Do you think that people grow from the bottom up, or from the top down?"

"From the top. I saw a column of soldiers yesterday, and some were taller than others at the top, but they were all equal at ground level."

"Not true. they grow from the bottom. After all, when you grow, your trousers get shorter from the bottom, not from the top."

✯ ✯ ✯

"Did you ever wonder whether it's the sugar or the stirring which makes tea sweet?"

"What a silly question, it's the sugar of course."

"Really? And did you ever drink unstirred tea? Well, was it sweet?"

"All right, but in that case why do people use sugar?"

"To find out how long they have to stir."

✯ ✯ ✯

"You ass!" says one friend to another.

"Perhaps I really am an ass, but let me think, am I an ass because I am your friend, or am I your friend because I am an ass?"

✯ ✯ ✯

"My cousin Srul has written me from South America that he manufactures suspenders. I don't get it!"

"What's not to understand?"

"Listen, here people wear suspenders so that their pants don't fall down, but in South America, on the reverse side of the globe, people walk upside down, so why do they need suspenders?"

"Don't you get it? Here we're in danger of our trousers falling down, but there they are in danger of falling out of their trousers!"

9

At The Doctor

An old Jew with a patriarchal beard comes to his doctor and starts to complain: "Doctor, nothing works any more. I get sharp pains in my heart, I get migraine headaches and dizzy spells. My liver is finished, my kidneys are falling apart, I can hardly see or hear, I have varicose veins and fallen arches. I can barely drag one foot behind the other, and on top of that I don't always feel very well."

✡ ✡ ✡

After getting a very strict diet from his doctor, the patient is trying to negotiate some exceptions.
"You say that beef is bad, but carp are healthy; are they?"
"I couldn't say. So far, I haven't examined any.

✡ ✡ ✡

Mrs. Rosenbaum is waiting to give birth. The gynecologist is playing cards with her husband next door.
Suddenly they hear a cry:
"Oh mon Dieu, que je souffre!" (French for "Oh my God, how I suffer!").
The husband springs to his feet, but the doctor assures him that it is not yet time, and they calmly resume their game.
After a while they hear another cry:
"Oh God, what pain!"
The husband again jumps up and the doctor again restrains him.
Suddenly she cries: "Oy vey! Mamele!" (Mummy!)

This time the doctor springs to his feet;
"Now it's time!"

✭ ✭ ✭

A patient comes to Sigmund Freud. To learn something about his patient, the scientist draws a circle and asks:
"With what do you associate this?"
"A female breast," replies the patient.
Freud draws a dot: "And this?"
"A nipple."
Freud next draws a triangle: "And this?"
"A mound of Venus."
The scientist puts away his pencil and cries: "You sir, are quite simply a pervert!"
"I'm a pervert? And who drew all those dirty pictures?"

✭ ✭ ✭

Aaron has a headache and wants to see the doctor.
"'Who needs a doctor to cure a stupid headache?" his wife demands.
"The poor doctor must live," Aaron says.
After seeing the doctor, he takes the prescription and sets out for the drug store.
"Do you really think that this medicine will help?" his wife sneers.
"The poor druggist also wants to live."
Aaron buys the medicine and throws it into the waste basket.
"Have you gone mad?" cries his wife. "Such expensive medicines!"
"My dear, I also want to live."

✭ ✭ ✭

Wasserzug is hard of hearing. The doctor advises him to stop drinking, as otherwise he might go deaf. The patient takes his advice, and soon there is great improvement. After a month, however, he has started to drink again, and is almost deaf.

"I warned you! Why didn't you take my advice?"

"Doctor, all the things I heard last month weren't worth a single glass of vodka!"

✯ ✯ ✯

The doctor whispers into a married woman's ear: "Your husband is very pale and nervous. I don't like the way he looks today."

"I haven't liked the way he looks from the moment I met him."

✯ ✯ ✯

Ruben the painter has a fever. A doctor is called. He takes the pulse and says with great assurance:

"Scarlet Fever."

"Impossible," Ruben replies. "I'm seventy years old and I've already had scarlet fever as a child."

"Oh? But look at your hands, see how red they are."

"That's paint. I'm a painter."

"Then you're very lucky, because if you were not a painter this would definitely be scarlet fever."

✯ ✯ ✯

An old Jew comes to an eye doctor because his eyesight is getting weak.

The doctor shows him a chart with letters, but it is evident that the patient knows only the Hebrew alphabet. He takes out a prayer book and orders the patient to read while gradually stepping back from the book. The patient keeps reading. The doctor is already ten feet away and the patient still reads without difficulty.

"But my dear sir, your eyesight is excellent."

"What has this to do with eyesight?" asks the patient. "Who's reading?"

✡ ✡ ✡

"Doctor, my ears are stuffed full of wax and I can hardly hear a thing"

The doctor turns on his little lamp and looks into one of the ears.

"You won't see right through," the patient warns. "The other ear is also blocked."

✡ ✡ ✡

"Doctor, my whole body hurts when I move my hands. In particular, when I raise my right arm while the left one is twisted down to the left, the pain drives me crazy."

"Then why do you do such advanced gymnastics?"

"And how else can I put my coat on?"

✡ ✡ ✡

A doctor is advising a habitual thief on how much medicine to take for his illness: "Take one spoon every two hours."

"A tin spoon or a silver one?"

"Either."

"I ask because I already took a dozen silver ones, but what difference will this make to my health?"

✡ ✡ ✡

The rabbi of a very poor kahal becomes consumptive. The doctor recommends walks and fresh milk. The neighborhood leaders discuss this, and then send a delegation to the rabbi.

"We've already gathered all the necessary funds for the walks, but we still can't afford the milk."

✡ ✡ ✡

First entry from the notebook of a village doctor: "There are two absolutely sure remedies for yellow fever. Neither is reliable."

Second entry: "There's one really creative remedy for a sore tooth: sit in a warm pair of trousers on a cold stove. It doesn't help the tooth, but neither does it any harm, and it costs nothing!"

✡ ✡ ✡

Old Rosencrantz is lying on his death bed. He calls his wife and children so that he can dispose of his estate.

"My oldest son Chaim is to inherit all my books.

"What for does he need the books? Let Libel get the books," interrupts his wife.

"Libel will get my suits, and my sheepskin," Rosencrantz goes on stubbornly.

"Chaim needs them more than Libel," his wife interjects.

"And I leave the family silver to Havel..."

"Havel is still so young, shouldn't Sarah get it instead?"

At this, Rosencrantz raises himself on his elbows and says to his wife: "Listen, who's dying here anyway, you or I?"

10

A Perfect Match

In nineteenth century Poland, many marriages were arranged by marriage brokers (shadchans).

✡ ✡ ✡

A shadchan addresses a young man: "I have a perfect match for you."
 "I'm not interested."
 "But you don't even know what she's like. She's a beauty!"
 "I'm not looking for beauty."
 "Ah, you want a good family? I can recommend one."
 "No.'"
 "I understand, you are a realist. I know a girl with a dowry of. .."
 "Just leave me alone. I'll marry only for love!"
 "No need to shout. You want love? I have a large choice of that as well."

✡ ✡ ✡

Goldfield, the banker, has a very unattractive daughter. One day, a shadchan comes to offer his services.
 "I have a great match for your daughter!"
 "I don't like your young man, he looks suspicious to me."
 "But you haven't even seen him."
 "It is enough to know that he wants to marry her."

✡ ✡ ✡

The daughter of a tycoon falls in love, and soon afterwards announces her engagement. The local shadchan visits the rich man and grumbles:

"How could you forget about your old, reliable match-maker?"

"I didn't need to take up your time," the father replies. "This marriage has been fashioned by Amor himself" (Amor is the god of Love).

"By Amor?" says the bewildered old man. "He must be from another town."

✿ ✿ ✿

The young man who is looking for a wife is a dreadful boaster. The shadchan warns him: "Don't exaggerate when you're talking to her parents. It makes a bad impression. If I see that you are galloping too far, I will give you a sign."

The visit is going well, and the conversation is flowing nicely. The young man, however, gets carried away, and says: "My uncle in America has a manor house in which the ballroom is one hundred meters long."

The shadchan kicks him under the table.

"And half a meter wide" finishes the candidate.

✿ ✿ ✿

A shadchan is trying to overcome the arguments of a romantic young man.

"So you don't believe in match-making? You think that you should marry only for love? Listen, I know a girl who's as pretty as an angel, and who will get a large dowry. She is an only daughter, and her father owns two factories and a bank. On top of that, he is a millionaire, and she'll be his only heir. Don't you think that she is the sort of girl with whom an enterprising young man like you could fall in love at first sight?"

"What are you saying? She walks with a terrible limp!"

"There's no need to raise your voice. Just think! What happens if you marry a healthy girl who falls and breaks her leg? Tears, lamentations, doctors, nurses, traction, plaster casts! Nothing but costs, grief and inconvenience! And here you'd have a partner who's gone through all that hassle already!"

✿ ✿ ✿

Young Cohen is musing: "I want a girl so beautiful that I would wish to marry her even without a dowry, and yet so rich that it wouldn't matter how she looked."

✡ ✡ ✡

A shadchan tells a doctor what a pity it is that he had not married.
 The doctor replies: "No, marriage is full of risks. If I marry a young girl, she'll be like an unwritten page. Who knows what devils are hiding in her? And a divorcee? She's already proved with her first husband that no man can live with her. A widow? Who knows how her husband bit the dust! But if you can find me a married woman who's kept her husband happy for a few years, I'd be very interested."

✡ ✡ ✡

In their time, the Brodsky family in Russia was as rich as the Rothschilds. One day, a shadchan appears before Brodsky and says:
 "I have an exceptional match for your daughter."
 The banker is visibly agitated by the news. "But my dear sir, my daughter does not need a match-maker to find a husband."
 "You'll change your mind when you learn who the party is," smiles the shadchan.
 "I'm all ears," says the banker, amused.
 "It's the Tsarevitch, the heir to the throne of Russia."
 Brodsky is astounded and not sure whether to take the offer seriously.
 At last he says: "If you can effect this union, then I agree."
 The shadchan leaves rubbing his hands with satisfaction, thinks a while and murmurs: "I'm halfway there. now for the Tsar!"

✡ ✡ ✡

Poor Goldbaum is blind, but that does not cool his ardor for marriage. His tastes lean towards the very ample. The shadchan searches far and wide for a suitable match. The poor man sets out to "look" at his future wife with his hands. He stretches them farther and farther, until he cries out in happy disbelief: "Is all this still my fiancée?"

✭ ✭ ✭

Father to son: "A man shouldn't marry a pauper's daughter!"
 "But father, I love that girl!"
 "Love, love! Do I have anything against love? But why love a pauper's daughter?"

✭ ✭ ✭

"I want you to marry Silverman's daughter," says a father to his son.
 "But father! I can be happy only with Miss Sulkier."
 "And once you're happy, then what?"

✭ ✭ ✭

"Father, I'd like to marry Miss Rosenberg. She is lovely and comes from a good family, but she has no money."
 "Well, one can't always have everything in life. So how much does this lady have?"
 "But I have just told you quite clearly, she has no money at all."
 "That's too much! It's not a crime to have no money. I can understand no money, but no money at all?"

✭ ✭ ✭

A student makes a grab at the rabbi's daughter, and she pushes him away indignantly. The young man wants to leave gracefully: "Oh well, if you don't want ..."
 "Of course I want; I'm just taken aback by your impudence!"

✭ ✭ ✭

"Mendel asked me for my hand," says Rifkin to her mother.

"And do you like this Mendel?" asks the mother tenderly.

"I do, even though he holds some strange views. For instance, he doesn't believe In hell."

"Trust me my dear, after he marries you, he will."

✺ ✺ ✺

A Jew advertises in the newspapers that he has three daughters of marriageable age, and that each of them will get a substantial dowry.

Soon a candidate arrives, and the father explains:

"My youngest daughter is twenty years old, and will get a dowry of $20,000. The second is thirty years old and will get $30,000, and the third is forty years old and will get $40,000."

The candidate thinks, sighs, scratches his head, and asks: "Do you have anything for 60 thousand?"

✺ ✺ ✺

"My new partner is a bit strange, he wants to have everything he looks at," says Yankel to a friend.

"Good. I'll have to introduce him to my eldest daughter."

✺ ✺ ✺

11

Married Bliss

"Darling, Sarit says to her husband, "On our wedding day you told me that I was your whole world."

"That's true my love, but I've learned some geography since then."

"Why don't you get married?" asks a friend.

"I have no luck with girls. When I find one who can cook like mother, she looks like my father. When she loves to sing like my mother, she's tone deaf like my father, And when I finally find one who cooks like my mother, knows business like my father, looks like an angel, and sings like a nightingale, she's just like my aunt Rifkin."

"But I've never even heard that you have an aunt Rifkin."

"That is the pity of it, neither have I."

✡ ✡ ✡

Darling," Ruth says to her husband, "I have to tell you that soon there will be three of us."

"How wonderful! But are you sure?"

"Absolutely! I've just received a letter from my mother, and it says that she's coming next week."

✡ ✡ ✡

"Doctor. I would like you to help my husband."

"What's wrong with him?"

"He talks in his sleep."

"I understand. You'd like a medicine to stop him from talking?"

"No! I'd like a medicine to make him speak more clearly.

✡ ✡ ✡

Moriz wakes from a nightmare in a cold sweat, and cries: "Sarah, my dear wife!"

"What?" she asks sleepily.

"Remember that pogrom in Russia? Were you with me then?"

"Of course I was. It was our wedding night. Now go to sleep."

Two hours later Moriz wakes with a cry, and grabs Sarah by the arm:

"And do you remember Crystal Night? Were you with me then?"

"Moriz, what's wrong with you, we were together, and we already had two children."

Moriz falls into a fitful sleep, from which he wakes screaming, and shakes his wife by the shoulders.

"And during the war, when we had to flee from the Germans across the mountains, were you with me?"

"But dear, you know very well that I never deserted you and that I was always by your side."

"So it is you who has brought me all that bad luck!"

✶ ✶ ✶

Marriage can be like a town under siege. Those who are outside are doing their best to get in, while those who are in are just dying to get out.

✶ ✶ ✶

"I have a wonderful wife, a real jewel. I hope she lives to be ninety nine."

"And why not a hundred?"

"Be reasonable! I'd like to live a little too."

✶ ✶ ✶

Steinberg meets his friend Zitrinbaum on Monday morning in the district of pleasure. His friend is visibly abashed.

"What are you doing here?" he asks.

"My wife's in a convalescence home, and I thought that this is my only chance to… you know."

"I understand. But what are you carrying under your arm?"

"My prayer book."

"You're kidding! What will you do with a prayer book?"

"I thought that if this really turns out to be fun, I may stay here till the Sabbath."

✡ ✡ ✡

A rabbi asks Yankel to see him: "People have reported to me that you're living in concubinage," he accuses.

"In concubinage? And what does that mean?"

"It means that you're living with another woman as you might do with your wife."

"That's not true. My life with her is much, much better."

✡ ✡ ✡

A Jewish woman is weeping because her daughter gave birth to a child only five months after her wedding.

"What shame! What dishonor!" she laments.

Her friends are trying to console her. One of them says:

"Relax; I think that her birth was timed properly, and that it was the wedding which was too late."

And the second friend adds: "At least it won't happen again."

✡ ✡ ✡

"Mister Katz, you often go to Paris for a week on business. How much do your journeys cost?"

"A thousand franks if I go with my wife. Four thousand if I go by myself."

✭ ✭ ✭

The first-time father sends a telegram to his in-laws: "Rebecca has happily born us a son."

Later, the father-in-law takes him aside, and says:

"How could you waste so much money on all those needless words in your telegram? Every word costs! See for yourself: you write 'Rebecca.' Who else could it be? Would you have sent us a telegram if it were not Rebecca? And then 'happily.' Does a man send a telegram if a birth was not happy? And then 'born.' Well, what else was she supposed to do after nine months of pregnancy? And finally 'a son,' would you send a telegram if the child was a daughter? Couldn't you have crossed all those words out?"

✭ ✭ ✭

Apfelbaum returns home unexpectedly, and finds his wife in the arms of his book-keeper. He goes to his office and tells his cashier to pay his dismissed book-keeper three months wages.

"Three months at 200 zlotys is 600 zlotys," the cashier calculates.

"Pay him 590 zlotys."

"What's the deduction for?"

"He'll know."

✭ ✭ ✭

"God has only just taken your beloved wife, and you're already taking another one!"

"Why not? If God can take, why not I?"

✭ ✭ ✭

Sarah looks at herself carefully in the mirror. At last she says with deep satisfaction: "I really don't envy my husband."

12

Parents And Children

Father: "Be careful what you say. God is omnipresent."
Son: "So what's He doing in this tram on the Sabbath?"

✡ ✡ ✡

A girl becomes pregnant, and her parents are going out of their minds to find the culprit. At last, she names the pious old rabbi. The parents cannot believe this, but the girl is adamant. Finally, the scandalous accusation reaches the rabbi, who summons all of them.

"How can you say such things about me?" he says, "I've never seen you in my life."

"It's true," the girl insists. "Don't you remember? Some months ago, when my childless aunt came to you for help; you gave her a bottle of water from the river Jordan to help her conceive? From curiosity, I took a swig from that bottle."

"But my child," says the old man, touched by her naiveté and innocence, "to conceive, you need the presence of a man."

"But I remember quite clearly that at least one man was present when I drank that water!"

✡ ✡ ✡

Horrified mother: "Our Esther may be pregnant!"

Father: "Impossible, we took the strictest precautions!"

Mother: "True, but don't forget that a student lived with us for a week."

Father: "Yes, but he had his own bed."

Mother: "True, but he could have gone over to her bed."

Father: "Yes, but we put up a screen between their beds, so he could not get into hers."

Mother: "Unless he walked around the screen."

Father: "Unless he did."

✡ ✡ ✡

A lot of works were written about Jewish mothers (Yiddishe mame). They are prepared to sacrifice everything for their children, and they expect such devotion to be requited.

One Yiddishe mame is consoling her friend, whose son has just been diagnosed as having, an "Oedipus complex":

"Who cares what they call his complex! The main thing is that he loves his mom."

✡ ✡ ✡

Little Moshe looks through the window, and sees the mailman with a heavy bag. "What are you carrying?" he asks.

"Letters."

"If they're so heavy, why don't you just send them by mail?"

✡ ✡ ✡

Rami calls on his friend Nathan, and asks him to come out and play soccer with him and the boys.

"Not today," says Rami. "I want to see a movie at six o'clock."

"That still leaves you three hours to play with us."

"You don't know my mother. It will take me three hours of crying and pleading before she allows me to see the movie."

✡ ✡ ✡

A son is about to embark on a journey to explore the world and search for happiness. His father says farewell:

"Go with God, my son."

"Father, do you really think that He will travel fourth class just to keep me company?"

✡ ✡ ✡

Motke's mother takes him to his first concert. He sees a conductor and a singer.

"Mother, why is he threatening her with his stick?"

"He's not threatening her," whispers the mother," He's conducting."

"Then why is she howling?"

✡ ✡ ✡

From Itzhak's first essay about woodpeckers:

"A woodpecker lives in the hollow of a tree. He loves the female woodpecker because she gives him broods of children who are quite bare and naked. To start with they have nothing but two ends: the long end and the short end. The long end is their beak, and the short end is their other end."

✡ ✡ ✡

"Grandpa, why are the rich so selfish?

The old man takes his granddaughter to the window and asks: "What do you see?" "People in the street."

"Good, come to the mirror. Now what do you see?"

"Myself."

"Both the window and the mirror are made of glass. You see other people when you look through clear glass, but when you sprinkle it with a bit of silver you see only yourself. And so it is with all people who have a little silver."

✡ ✡ ✡

Two fathers meet and start talking about their sons:

"Whenever I get a letter from mine, I reach out for a dictionary of foreign words," says the first.

"And I reach for my check book," says the other.

✲ ✲ ✲

An old Jew is boasting to his friend that he has four sons, all of whom are educated, and all of whom move in the highest circles of the intelligentsia.

"And who are your sons?"

"One is a doctor, the second is a lawyer, the third is a writer, and the fourth is a professor."

"And you, what do you do?"

"I have a little business which, thank God, makes enough to keep all of us alive."

✲ ✲ ✲

Old Rubinstein is explaining the mystery of economics to his son:

"Remember, everything that is rare is expensive. For example, a good horse is a rarity, and is therefore expensive."

The son is not quite convinced: "But father, a good horse which is also cheap is even a greater rarity!"

✲ ✲ ✲

13

How's Business?

Old Rosenzweig is about to die. He dictates the names of all his debtors to his sons, after which he falls exhausted on his pillows.

"And what about our creditors" asks one of his sons.

"Don't worry, they'll find you soon enough."

✧ ✧ ✧

The owner of a firm thinks that his accountant spends too much when traveling on business, and asks him to explain all of his expenses for his latest trip. The accountant presents a detailed list:

Travel	10,000
Breakfast	2,000
Taxis	4,000
Dinner	5,000
Hotel	11,000
Man is not made of wood	80,000

The owner can hardly believe his eyes:

"Mister Rosenblum," he says, "I understand that Man is not made of wood, but neither is he made of stainless steel!"

✧ ✧ ✧

A merchant tells his wife to burn bright lights when his affairs are going poorly and to burn a solitary little candle when they are going well. He explains:

"When things go badly for us, let the others eat their hearts out, and they will do so if they think that we are doing well. But when things are going well, I'll give others the consolation of thinking that I am down to my last candle!"

✫ ✫ ✫

Business is bad and Ethan is despondent. "What'll I do? How will I live?"

"Wheat is good business now," says a friend. "Why don't you buy wheat?"

"How can I buy wheat when I don't have any cash?"

"Then rent out your warehouse."

"What warehouse? My creditors got it long ago."

"Too bad. But could you sell your furniture? You should get a hundred for that."

"What furniture? I'm sitting in an empty house."

"My dear fellow, this means that you are bankrupt!"

"So that's what bankruptcy looks like?"

✫ ✫ ✫

"My accountant who stole my money, and then ran away with my daughter is already regretting it."

"He returned your money?"

"No, my daughter."

✫ ✫ ✫

The owner of a business is reading the paper, and says to his accountant: "Rosenberg's cashier ran off with 100,000 rubles. We must settle our accounts. How much do you think we lost?"

"Nothing. We have not traded with Rosenberg for months."

"Thank God. I see that Abramovitch in Berlin went broke. Did he owe us anything?"

"Not a kopeck."

"Bauscher's having difficulties. No one knows what could happen. How much do we have at risk?"

"Nothing," says the accountant, "We didn't deal with him at all."

At this, the owner flings down his newspaper angrily and shouts:"What's the meaning of all this? Do I have a business or don't I!?"

✡ ✡ ✡

A father takes his son on a business trip. Already during the first purchase, the son sees that his father is bargaining hard for every kopeck.

"Why all this haggling, why this charade?" he asks. "You have driven the price down to rock bottom, when we both know that you have no intention of paying anyway."

"That's true," sighs the father. "But I like the vendor. He's a nice man. When I don't pay, I want him to think that he lost a little bit less."

✡ ✡ ✡

"I'm in a tight spot, and I can't deal with all my problems. sighs a Jew.

"Don't worry, God will provide." replies a friend.

"I'm sure He will, but could you lend me five rubles till He does?"

✡ ✡ ✡

A guest says to the owner of a hotel:

"It's impossible to do business in this town. I've been here for two weeks, and so far I found only one honest person to deal with."

The hotel owner is intrigued:

"One honest person, you say? Now let me see, who on earth could that be?"

✫ ✫ ✫

At the stock exchange: "Be careful of that little scoundrel over there or he will pick your pockets."

"That's all right. In my time, I also started small."

✫ ✫ ✫

A manager says sternly to his cashier:

"It was reported to me that you steal from my cash box."

"I am loyal only to you. I wouldn't dream of stealing from anyone else."

✫ ✫ ✫

"My former partner, whom I engaged in my business when he was still a pauper, has swindled me out of one hundred thousand guldens, and is now sitting in America doing business with my money. Blackguard! Thief!"

"What are you saying? One shouldn't malign someone who has one hundred thousand guldens!"

✫ ✫ ✫

"I can't pay you to-day, but I swear that I'll pay next month. Please be patient, it will only take thirty days."

"Thirty days I can last, but thirty nights?"

✫ ✫ ✫

A certain Jew falls on hard times and decides to become a highway robber. He takes a big knife and goes into the forest. A Jewish peddler is the first to come along.

"Halt! Your money or your life!" cries the bandit.

"Oy vey! How you scared me! Stop fooling!"

"I'm not fooling! I'm a bandit. Give me what you have!"

"What do you mean? And what will my family live on? Do you want my poor babies to starve?"

"You're right. So give me twenty rubles!"

"How can you ask a poor junkman for twenty rubles?"

"Oh, all right. Then at least give me ten."

"How can you even ask for that? You want me to trade without capital? How could I buy new stock?"

"I see, I see. But do you at least have some tobacco?"

"I'm sure I could find some to share with a decent man in need."

"Good. Then please give a poor robber a sniff"

✡ ✡ ✡

A Jew from another town arrives for the local fair. He proclaims he's an acrobat, and that to-day he will dance on a tightrope stretched between the steeple of the church and the roof of the synagogue. He collects the entrance fee of 10 kopeks in advance.

At the appointed hour, a crowd begins to gather on the market square, while the acrobat is standing on the roof of the synagogue. Everyone holds their breath, as he turns to address the crowd.

"My dear brethren. I've never stood on a tightrope, and I don't know how to dance. And now, it's your decision; If you think that your 10 kopeks are worth my life, then I could give it a try."

✡ ✡ ✡

A clerk is running up and down the office shouting: "Oh, what a headache! I can't bear it! I'm losing my mind!"

"Mister Silverman," says the owner, "Go home if you are ill, but don't run around boasting that you have a mind."

✯ ✯ ✯

"How much are these trousers?" asks a client.

"We have fixed prices in our shop," says the owner. "That's why I won't ask for 20, or for 18, or for 16. But I'll certainly not sell them for less than 15 rubles."

To which the client replies:

"And I'll not offer you 5, or 7, or 9, but I'll certainly not buy them from you for more than 10 rubles."

"Wrap these trousers at once," says the owner to the sales assistant. "Please come again. It's nice to have a customer who doesn't try to haggle."

✯ ✯ ✯

A trader sold someone a lame horse. The buyer soon notices the defect and raises an alarm. A crowd gathers, shouting that this act was base, mean, and despicable!

"Such is this world of ours," says the embittered trader. "Everyone shouts about the one bad leg, but no one praises the three good ones!"

✯ ✯ ✯

The owner of an elegant men's shop in Warsaw would tell others:

"Our staff in this branch is having a very hard time. Although the business gives us just enough profit to live in luxury, to fund our children's education, to marry off our daughters to good parties, and to send our wives to world-famous health spas four times each year, it's almost impossible for us to pay our promissory notes."

✯ ✯ ✯

A factory owner is doing business in the city, when he accidentally spots his bookkeeper sitting in a barber's shop. Furious, he barges into the shop and shouts:

"What's going on? You dare to get your hair cut during working hours?"

"That's when it grew," is the calm reply.

✳ ✳ ✳

A shoemaker's wife reproaches her husband: "How could you give shoes to a complete stranger who doesn't have the cash to pay at once? Why should he bother to come back to pay you when he has the shoes already?"

"Because both shoes are for the left foot."

✳ ✳ ✳

Jewish author Shalom Aleichem explains the meaning of some business phrases:

"Things are going badly" means: "He's doing well, while I have losses."

"Things are not going badly" means: "We're both making profits."

"I'm doing well" means "I am making profits, and he is losing."

✳ ✳ ✳

"Mister Weisman, you never buy or sell a thing. Why did you come to market?"

"I was hoping that to-day I may be lucky and get a free ride home."

✳ ✳ ✳

14

In Court

The judge asks Silverman:

"So you claim that you paid two hundred rubles? The plaintiff denies this. Can you swear that you have really paid?"

"I think so" says the accused.

The judge objects: "No, this won't do. When you swear, you must say you either have paid or have not paid."

"If you put it that way, I can swear to that," says Silverman with relief

✡ ✡ ✡

Katz was caught breaking and entering and is facing the court:

"I can't understand one thing," says the judge. "Why did you steal worthless rubbish when that house is full of priceless things?"

"Oy your honor, please stop. I can't stand it! My wife has nagged me about this already, and now you are starting to do the same."

✡ ✡ ✡

Yankel is accused of stealing a sack full of turnips from his neighbor's field. He doesn't want to admit it:

"I really didn't steal. The night was as dark as pitch and it was very stormy. I wanted to take shelter from the wind, so I squatted in the field among the turnips. And the wind was so violent that it tore out the turnips from the soil."

If that is so, how did they get blown into the sack?"

"This has puzzled me since yesterday!"

✡ ✡ ✡

A thief was caught in the act and is in jail. He wants a good lawyer to defend him.

"And what could a defense lawyer possibly do to help you?" asks the policeman.

"That's what I'd like to find out," replies the thief

✻ ✻ ✻

Simon and Zeke were good friends till the day when Zeke borrowed two hundred rubles from Simon, and did not pay them back. When Simon takes his friend to court, Zeke denies ever borrowing the money. Simon is not able to prove his case. As they leave the court together, Simon says bitterly:

"Aren't you ashamed to commit perjury for two hundred rubles?"

"And aren't you ashamed to force your best friend to commit perjury for such a trifling sum?"

✻ ✻ ✻

A man was asked to come to court as a witness. To his annoyance the judge keeps referring to him as the butcher. At one point the witness can stand it no longer:

"With the court's permission, I'm not just a butcher: I am a cantor to my community, I am a melamed to the children, and I'm a butcher only to cattle."

✻ ✻ ✻

A lawyer who is interviewing his client is not getting very far. "Mister Cohen did you or did you not swindle your partner?"

"Mister Lawyer, do I look like a man who would swindle his partner?"

"Well, did you or did you not forge the signature on this bill?"

"Mister Lawyer, do I look like a man who would forge the signature on a bill?"

"Mister Cohen, why do you keep answering my questions with questions of your own?"

"Mister Lawyer, do I look like a man who would answer your questions with questions of my own?"

15

Travel

"When we were traveling through the forest last night, we were surrounded by a hundred wolves."
"Incredible! A hundred wolves?"
"Well, and even if there were only fifty or twenty, isn't that enough?"
"So there were twenty?"
"I don't see why you should insist on such accurate numbers. Surely, even one wolf is a great danger."
"Of course! Was it really a wolf?"
"It must have been. What else would growl like that in the undergrowth?"

✣ ✣ ✣

"Last year, I was attacked by ninety nine wolves in a forest."
"You had time to count them?"
"No, but if I said 'one hundred' you'd think I was exaggerating."

✣ ✣ ✣

The owner of a tavern is showing a traveler to his room. The guest takes one look at it and says with disgust:
"But the walls are crawling with bedbugs!"
"And what did you expect, brown bears?"

✣ ✣ ✣

Conversation: "So you come from Zlotoryja? I used to live there. What an awful town. I don't remember one decent person from there.

"What nonsense! I could list at least a dozen with one breath."

"For example..."

"Well, there is.... then there is... umm... Must they actually come from Zlotoryja?

✡ ✡ ✡

"Did you sleep well last night?" asks the inn-keeper.

"I did, thank you, but the poor bedbugs didn't sleep a wink."

✡ ✡ ✡

The travelers are exasperated by the slow pace of Balagula's cart.
"Why should I drive my poor horses? Believe me, when they feel like it, they can pull like demons!"
"So why are they dragging their feet like in a funeral?"
"What can I do? When these horses feel like it they are magnificent! It's just that so far they never felt like it."

✡ ✡ ✡

Balagula grumbles about his nag:
"Devil take it! It's supposed to be as blind as Samson, but let there be the slightest hole or bump in the road, and it'll be sure to find it!"

✡ ✡ ✡

Itzhak runs panting into the station just as the train is leaving, and misses it.
"You anti-Semite," he mutters.

✡ ✡ ✡

"Where are you going to?" asks a man on a train.
"From Warsaw to Kovno."
"You don't say! I'm going from Kovno to Warsaw. Isn't modern technology wonderful, that we can both travel on the same train?"

✡ ✡ ✡

Two men are sitting opposite each other in a railway compartment. One introduces himself:
"Von Bedew, captain of the reserves."
"Rosenblum, still unfit for service."

✡ ✡ ✡

Tulpenrat thinks that the railway ticket costs too much and starts to haggle:

"You must give me a better deal."

The ticket seller gets angry: "This is not a bazaar! Pay the same price as everyone."

Tulpenrat does not give up, but the train pulls out.

"See, now we have both lost!"

✼ ✼ ✼

A Jew from the country comes to the Warsaw Zoo and sees his first giraffe. He looks at its long neck and mutters: "No, I still don't believe it!"

✼ ✼ ✼

"One third class ticket please."

"Where to?"

"In-Poznan."

"I don't have tickets for In-Poznan, only To-Poznan."

"Then just give me one To-Poznan and I'll walk the rest."

✼ ✼ ✼

Talk on a train:

"Do you know that our chazan Rosenblum from Odessa earns twenty thousand rubles a year?"

"Can that be true?"

"Absolutely," says a third passenger, "Except that he lives in Yalta and not Odessa, he is a merchant and not a chazan, and instead of earning twenty thousand he loses them."

✼ ✼ ✼

A traveler's car breaks down in a small town in Podole. He tries to start it by himself without success. He finds the local jack-of-all-trades who arrives with a hammer. He lifts the hood, takes one glance at the motor, and taps it gently in one spot. The car starts at once. The traveler is overjoyed but frowns when he sees the bill for 20 zlotys. "So much? Please explain it in detail," he asks.

He then gets the following bill: "I tapped   I zloty
I knew where to tap... 19 zlotys."

✫ ✫ ✫

16

In The East

Poland was partitioned in 1796 by Prussia, Austria, and Russia who occupied Eastern Poland till 1918. The Tsar resettled many Jews from Russia to the occupied territories

✡ ✡ ✡

Shortly before the Russian Revolution a Jew faces the court for calling the Tsar an ass. Terrified, he swears that the man he called an ass was Austria's Emperor Wilhelm II.
  "Don't lie! When people call someone an ass, we know exactly which ass they have in mind!"

✡ ✡ ✡

After the Russian Revolution a teacher giving a lesson, without thinking, says: "And God gave the raven a piece of cheese."
  A pupil rises and says; "But there is no God."
  "And is there cheese?" asks the teacher thinking quickly.
  "No."
  "As you see, I was using a figure of speech."

✡ ✡ ✡

A well-known free-thinker is dancing joyfully during the feast of Sachet Torah. When someone asks him if he is celebrating the wisdom in the Torah, he replies:

"No, I'm just glad that the Tsar's police were not asked to enforce its laws!"

✡ ✡ ✡

A Russian officer opens the door of a train compartment in which some Jews are sitting. He looks haughtily around and says: "I'd give a thousand rubles to find a place in which there isn't a single Jew."

"Just go to any Russian cemetery," someone suggests.

✡ ✡ ✡

It was difficult to leave the Soviet Union. A Jew applies for permission to go to Israel.

"What is your profession, comrade?" asks the official.

"Engineer." says the applicant.

"We can't allow you to leave! You could betray important professional secrets."

"But comrade, let's be serious. Science and technology in the U.S.S.R. are decades behind the capitalist countries."

"That's one of the secrets."

✡ ✡ ✡

Comrade Ivanov meets Abramovitch on the street:

"You don't look too well today. Did something happen?"
"A catastrophe. They threw me out of the Party for the third time."
"You don't say! What for?"
"They threw me out the first time after Stalin's funeral. When the party secretary told us that it cost fifty million rubles, I blurted out that for that money we could have buried the whole Party. They took me back after I submitted a self-criticism."

"They threw me out the second time when Malenkov replaced Khrushchev. The secretary came into my office, took one look at the portraits on the wall and said: "Remove that son-of-a-b..."
"Which one?" I asked.

"They reinstated me after another self-criticism. After that everything went well until last week. Through bad luck the secretary met me on the street and asked: 'Why were you absent from the last meeting of our branch committee?' "I said that had I known that this would be our last meeting, I would have come for certain."

✡ ✡ ✡

Shlomo is trying to deepen his understanding of communism: "Rebbe, what is an industrial reorganizer?"
"A clever man who thinks out new ways to meet our production targets."
"Rebbe and what is a Stakhanovite."
"A man who makes us feel guilty by working harder and longer than others."
"Rebbe and what is Pravda?"
"A newspaper named after (May God forgive them) The Truth."
"Rebbe and what is a Party Secretary?"
"Shlomo, stop bothering me with such questions. The longer I listen to you, the more clearly I see that we'll have to emigrate.

✡ ✡ ✡

17

In The Army

World War I between the powers that partitioned Poland meant that Jews in opposing armies had to fight each other.

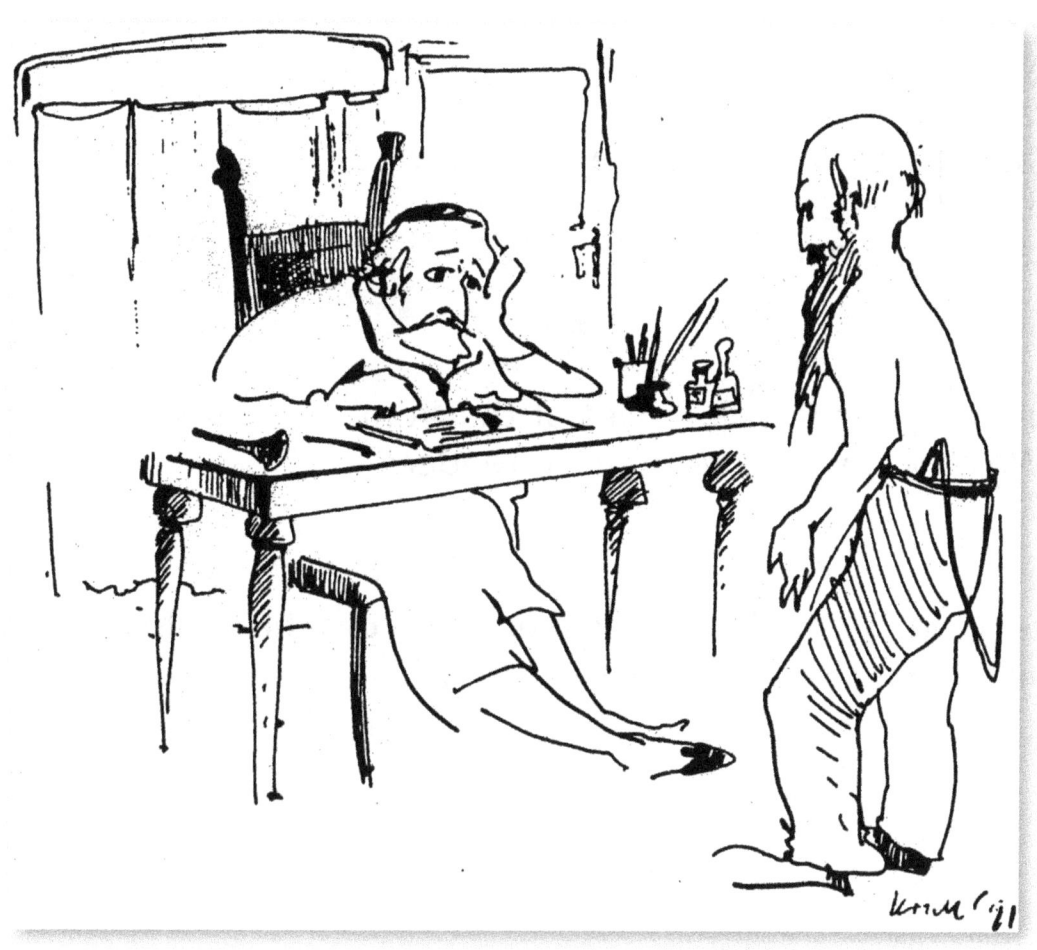

An army draft is taking place in a small town, in Tsarist Russia. Yankel is doing his best to evade it by convincing the doctor that he is not fit:

"Doctor, do you see that cockroach in the corner, by the table?"

The doctor wipes his glasses and gives a hard look.

"No, I see nothing in that corner."

"Over there, a bit closer to the broom."

"Well," says the doctor uncertainly, "I seem to see a darker spot."

"There you are," says Yankel. "And I can't see it at all!"

✧ ✧ ✧

Tsar Nicholas is inspecting his troops. He asks each soldier the same question:

"Why are you in service?"

"Because I love my Tsar," says one.

"Because I love my country," says the second.

"And you?" the Tsar asks Reuben,

"Because someone informed on me."

✧ ✧ ✧

A recruit in Tsarist Russia arrives at the front. He enters the trench and asks: "Which way would we go to surrender?"

✧ ✧ ✧

"Rosenbloom, why should a soldier gladly give his life for the Tsar?"

"I quite agree, sergeant, why should he?"

✧ ✧ ✧

The Emperor Francis Joseph asks a rabbi:
"Do you have sons?"
"By the grace of God, I do."
"And do they serve in the army?"
"By the grace of God, they don't."

✡ ✡ ✡

The sergeant is instructing recruits:
"I'll count to three, and then you will run like the wind. Attention! I'm starting now! One, two ...hey you! Why are you running? Didn't you understand the order?"
"Perfectly, but the others are asses. I knew at once that you'll say three."

✡ ✡ ✡

The captain is inspecting his troops: "Rosenblum, one of your buttons is missing!"
"Oy! I wish that all my problems were so big, captain!"

✡ ✡ ✡

A shell bursts near the trench with a mighty bang. Itzhak is shaken and indignant.
"Those damned German gunners! Don't they realize that there are people here?"

✡ ✡ ✡

Sergeant: "Why does a soldier have a gun?"
Itzhak: "So that, (God forbid), he could shoot from time to time."

✡ ✡ ✡

18

In Nazi Germany

After 1933, a beggar stands on a street corner in Germany. He has a card on his chest with: "Blind from birth. I accept nothing from Jews."

A passing Jew walks up to him and says indignantly: "I will give you five marks to remove that card at once!"

"Don't try to teach me. I know how to beg from those bandits!"

✡ ✡ ✡

A history teacher asks a pupil:
"Tell me, why did Germany lose the war in 1918?"
"Because of the Jewish generals," replies the child without hesitation.
"But there were no Jewish generals in the German army."
"That's why."

✡ ✡ ✡

A Jew presents himself to the recruitment center in London at the beginning of World War II. He had fled from Nazi Germany, and wants to fight.

"What is your name," asks a phlegmatic English officer.

"Wilhelm Adolph Deutch," replies the Jew.

"Tell me," the officer asks, slowly taking off his glasses, "aren't you exaggerating this a little?"

✡ ✡ ✡

A Jew hears a cry for help from a man drowning in a canal. He dives in and pulls the man out. It is Adolph Hitler.

"You have saved my life! How can I ever thank you? I will do anything you ask."

"Don't tell my neighbors."

19

From All Over The World

An old Jew from Morocco is visiting his grandson in Paris. He sees the underground metro for the first time in his life, and is amazed that the trains move by themselves. He examines them with great interest and finally asks:
"But where are the beasts of burden?"
"Sitting in the carriages."

✡ ✡ ✡

A pious old Jew arrives in Warsaw and asks a passer-by on the street:
"I'm looking for goldsmith Rosenzweig on Bialostocka Street. Could you please tell me how to find him?"
"What do you mean Rosenzweig? Goldsmith Rosenzweig doesn't live in Warsaw but in Odessa. Our goldsmith is called Rosenbaum, but he doesn't live on Bialostocka. You take the number 10 tram to the last stop, get out and go North till you reach the Greek Orthodox church with a dome like an onion. Turn left and walk a further twenty minutes, till you come to a small dead-end street without a name. There, in the third house on the left, lives a blind man who makes a living weaving wicker baskets. Rosenbaum doesn't live with him, but above him, next to a shoemaker who has a club foot, and who has been suffering from bunions for twenty years. Rosenbaum has rented out a room there on the eleventh of December two years ago, but if you want to find out if the shoemaker is still suffering from his bunions, you'll have to ask some other passer-by."

✡ ✡ ✡

A rich Jewish merchant from the country goes to a nearby town on business. He is wearing a shabby suit which is torn in many places. An acquaintance spots him and asks:

"Aren't you embarrassed to walk about this town in such rags?"

"Why should I be embarrassed? Nobody here has any idea who I am,"

A few weeks later, the same acquaintance meets the same merchant in his own village, and he is still wearing the same suit.

"Your dress is as slovenly as the one you wore in town," says the acquaintance.

"And why shouldn't it be? Everybody here knows me."

A large new McDonald's restaurant was built opposite the synagogue in New York. One day, the shammes sees a fat man with a cigar in his teeth, leaving a bar and making his way to the synagogue. He wants to see the rabbi on important business.

The shammes is nosy by nature, and eavesdrops on the conversation. Only occasional fragments reach his ears:

"I'll donate 100,000 dollars to the synagogue."
"I can't accept."
"200,000 dollars."
"Out of the question."
"500,000 dollars!"
"Absolutely not!"

The fat man leaves, angrily slamming the door. The shammes runs to his rabbi: "What are you doing rebbe? how can you refuse so much money for our Synagogue?"

"And do you have any idea what he wanted us to do?" asks the rabbi.

"I didn't hear."

"With the exception of holidays, he wanted us to end our prayers not with "amen" but with "McDonald's.""

✡ ✡ ✡

A representative of the tax authorities is questioning a young artist at the exhibition of his paintings in Montparnasse:

"What prices do your paintings command?"
"Between two and three million francs."
"Then why didn't you declare this in your income tax returns?"
"Because no one has bought any in the last six years."

✡ ✡ ✡

Two Jews see a Black American reading a book in Yiddish on a New York train. They look at each other and nod their heads. Then, one of them whispers to the reader:

"Do you really need this? Don't you have enough trouble already?"

✡ ✡ ✡

It is Spain, during the darkest hours of the Inquisition. Two Jewish friends can no longer resist the pressure, and decide to be baptized. They arrive at the cathedral and ask for an audience with the cardinal. He's absent, so they decide to wait. An hour passes, and then another until it is late afternoon. One of the would-be converts turns to the other and says:

"Unless the cardinal comes here soon, we'll be late for our evening devotions in the synagogue."

✡ ✡ ✡

A new young rabbi always travels to his synagogue on his bicycle. He leaves it propped against the wall.

One day, the bicycle disappears. There is little doubt about it, someone must have stolen it, and the thief must have been one of the faithful. Calling the police is out of the question, for he could not admit that one of his sheep has strayed. The young shepherd turns for advice to a revered old rabbi who is famous for his wisdom. The old man praises his discretion, and suggests:

"This Sabbath you will be teaching about the Ten Commandments. When you come to 'thou shalt not steal,' look into the eyes of the faithful. The thief is sure to feel remorse. He'll return the bicycle, and you will show him your mercy and forgiveness."

The young rabbi is impressed by the wisdom and the kindness of the old man's advice.

A few weeks later, the old rabbi sees the young one riding on his bicycle. He is overjoyed and calls out: "So you took my advice?"

"I did, rebbe."

"You recited the Ten Commandments, and everything went as I foresaw?"

"Not quite, rebbe. Just as I reached 'thou shalt not commit adultery' I suddenly remembered where I had left my bicycle."

✡ ✡ ✡

A visitor in New York sees a signboard: **HOW TO MAKE MONEY**. Intrigued, he goes inside.

"What sort of advice do you give?"

"All sorts of advice. My fees are 1 dollar, 5 dollars, 10 dollars, even 100 dollars."

"Very well, here is 1 dollar."

"A bus fare costs 10 cents. You will save this every time you walk."

"But every child knows that," says the visitor.

"So what do you expect for a dollar?"

"Well then, what can you give me for 5 dollars?"

"The shop round the corner is having a sale. You can buy things at half price."

"That's better! Here's 100 dollars, now tell me, how can I make real money?"

"Give advice!"

✫ ✫ ✫

A Jewish visitor finds a kosher restaurant in Paris. He is greeted by a Chinese waiter, who addresses him in fluent Yiddish:

"Good evening sir, please take a seat. Here's your menu."

The visitor is enchanted. The owner of the restaurant, with a traditional beard then arrives to ask if the service is good.

"Excellent, wonderful," assures the client." But I must confess that I'm amazed at how well your waiter speaks Yiddish."

"Not so loud please;"says the owner glancing around, "This man works here since last month and he still thinks he's learning French."

✫ ✫ ✫

The life of Jewish writers after the War was hard. One of them writes in a daily newspaper, and is paid by the word.

One day, the editor calls him after reading his last report.

"This paragraph is very strange." He reads aloud: The driver cracked his whip and called out: 'Giddy up! Giddy up! Giddy up! Giddy up!' Why so many Giddy ups?"

"Can I help it if the horse didn't want to start?"

✯ ✯ ✯

Moshe meets Yankel, who is strolling with a roll of newspapers under his arm.

"What are you reading?" he asks. Yankel shows him the papers and Moshe is shocked to see that they are all anti-Semitic. He cannot hide his outrage.

"Try to understand" explains Yankel. "When I buy Jewish papers, all I read about is how Jews are ill treated, lynched and oppressed. In short, nothing but despair. But in these papers I learn that Jews rule the world, that they control Manhattan, that the Swiss banks are in their hands that they have all the key positions in the Polish government, that they monopolize trade with the East, and that the arms industry is in their hands. Would such news not raise your spirits?"

✯ ✯ ✯

The Goldenberg's arrive at the hotel on the Azure Coast where they spend their annual vacations.

On this occasion however, they stay only one night, after which they pack and go to the desk. The receptionist informs the owner, and he comes running at once.

"Dear mister and madam Goldenberg! You are leaving already? What happened? Was the service in any way less than perfect?"

"Sir, please give us the bill," replies Goldenberg frostily.

"Of course, of course, since you have decided to leave. But tell me at least, why are you leaving?"

"Do you want to know the truth?"

"Of course, mister Goldenberg."

"Very well, we were told that you are an anti-Semite."

"But my dear mister Goldenberg! Would I be an anti-Semite in the middle of the high season?"

✲ ✲ ✲

The great Viennese actor Sonnenthal went to a cafe, and sat down at a table with a stranger. When the waiter came, the stranger placed his order with a pronounced stutter:

"P-p-please b-b-ring me a c-coffee."

"P-p-please b-b-ring one f-for m-me too," said Sonnenthal.

"B-but I have-seen you o-on the s-stage, and you d-don't s-s-tutter."

"I s-s-t-tutter quite often, it is only on s-stage that I p-prêt-tend that I don't."

✲ ✲ ✲

A rich woman orders a portrait by Lieberman. She asks the painter whether the portrait will be her true likeness.

"I will paint it so that the portrait will look more like yourself than you do in real life," replies the painter.

✲ ✲ ✲

To a woman who spoke interminably during a portrait sitting, Lieberman said: "Another word, madam, and I'll paint you exactly as you are."

✫ ✫ ✫

The painter Lesser Uri was friendly with Lieberman for many years, but later they quarreled. One day, someone told Lieberman that Uri was boasting about one of his paintings, which was really painted by Lieberman.

"I don't mind, so long as he is boasting that he has painted one of my pictures. But if he ever starts boasting that I painted one of his pictures, I'll sue!"

✫ ✫ ✫

During a visit to the United States, a Zionist leader was asked what he thought of American Jews.

"After all those meetings, I got the impression that Christopher Columbus was the only American Jew who did not start his career delivering newspapers or shining shoes."

✫ ✫ ✫

Weizmann, the first president of Israel, complained to President Truman:

"My job is much harder than yours. You are merely the president of one hundred and fifty million Americans, but I have to rule one million presidents."

✫ ✫ ✫

Einstein was one of the few who understood the Theory of Relativity. One day, he said:

"If my theory is ever proven to be correct, the Germans would say that I'm a German, and the French would call me a citizen of the world. If, on the other hand, it was proven to be wrong, the French would say that I was German, and the Germans would say that I was a Jew."

✫ ✫ ✫

Albert Einstein once met Charlie Chaplin, and said:

"What I admire most about your art is that it's so international. The whole world relates to it and understands it."

"That's true," said Chaplin. "But your fame is incomparable. Everybody admires you although no one understands you."

✻ ✻ ✻

Droyanov, the famous folklorist, once said to Chaim Bialik:
"I knew a marvelous story that I wanted to tell you, but I forgot it."
"Oh, when it comes to forgotten stories, I knew one that was even better!"

✻ ✻ ✻

"Why did Adam and Eve live so long?" "Because they had no In-laws."

✻ ✻ ✻

"Why should the men instead of the women provide for the household?"
"Because the first time a woman fed a man they lost their paradise."

✻ ✻ ✻

"Which war killed one quarter of the world's population?"
"The war between Cain and Abel."

✻ ✻ ✻

"Why do people never have what they want?"
"Because if they truly wanted what they had, they would have what they wanted, but they never want what they have, so they never have what they want."

✻ ✻ ✻

"What's the difference between the poor and the rich?"

"The poor think that money can get you everything. The rich know that it can't.

✧ ✧ ✧

"What is the heaviest burden to carry?"
"An empty wallet."

✧ ✧ ✧

"How can you tell a goose from a gander?"
"You throw down some bread. If she comes to eat it, that is the goose. If he comes to eat it, then that is the gander."

✧ ✧ ✧

"Why does a dog wag its tail?"
"Because it is stronger than the tail. If it wasn't, the tail would wag the dog."

✧ ✧ ✧

"It says here that water boils in a temperature of one hundred degrees Centigrade."
"Amazing! How does it know when it has reached one hundred?"

✧ ✧ ✧

What is the difference between a dictatorship and a democracy?
In a dictatorship the government does what it wants without listening to the people. In a democracy, the government listens to the people before it does what it wants.

✧ ✧ ✧

"How do you make a doughnut?"

"You take a hole, and form the dough around it."

✡ ✡ ✡

Two friends meet after five years and look on each other in silence. At last one of them says: "I haven't seen you for five years, and you don't even ask how things are?"
"Well, how are things?"
"Don't even ask!"

20

Israel

"Zionism's is a wonderful idea," says a lawyer. Personally, as soon as Israel is created, I would love to be its consul in New York."

✻ ✻ ✻

"Professor, what do you have against Zionists?"
 "Nothing in principle, except for a few small details. First of all, why did they choose Palestine? It's wet in the North and a desert in the South. Aren't there more scenic countries in the world? Secondly, why do they want to speak Hebrew, that old tongue which hardly anyone knows? And lastly, what made them choose the Jews? Is there a shortage of more congenial nations?"

✻ ✻ ✻

What is Zionism?
 "Zionism is when one Jew discusses with a second Jew, how to get money from a third one to send a fourth one to Palestine."

✻ ✻ ✻

During the War of Independence in 1948, they mobilized all the resources of the nation. An old man with a white beard was among those who presented themselves to the draft board as volunteers.
 "Grandpa, we can't take soldiers of your age."
 "What? You don't need generals?"

✻ ✻ ✻

One day, a famous conductor from New York came to give a symphonic concert in Tel Aviv. Yitzhak Ben-Zvi takes his place in the central loge with his wife, and with Pola and David Ben-Gurion.

After a few minutes, Pola turns to her husband and whispers:

"David... David, Iitzhak has fallen asleep."

"And to tell me that you wake me up?"

✡ ✡ ✡

The Minister of Finance is discussing the worsening economic and political picture in Israel with General Moshe Dayan.

"I have an idea," he says. "Why don't we declare war on the United States?" They will defeat us in no time, and we will become an American colony. They will then give us massive funds to rebuild our country, develop our economy, modernize our industry, and arm us with the latest weapons."

"That's all very well, but what if we win?"

✡ ✡ ✡

The efficiency of the Israeli Intelligence is justly renowned.

After the 1967 war which the Arabs lost, Nasser calls on his best agent for a special mission. He is to go to Israel, to find out the full military potential of the enemy. The agent is to fly into Tel Aviv as a Cypriot. There, he is to meet a contact from Cairo, who lives on Allenby Street under the false name of Rabinovitch.

The agent arrives, but finds out that three men called Rabinovitch live at that address, and that he must find the right one.

"I will have to use the secret pass-word," he thinks.

He rings the first bell, and an old Jew with a white beard appears. The agent says: "The Egyptian pyramids are among the wonders of the world."

"Ah," says the old man without a trace of surprise. "You're looking for Rabinovitch the spy! Second floor on the left."

✡ ✡ ✡

A native of Tel Aviv is about to make his first business trip to Paris. His neighbor thinks that this is a splendid idea, and explains:

"Paris is an extraordinary city. You will never meet more hospitable people. They wait for you at the station as you get off the train. They take you to exclusive restaurants and to luxurious hotels. Someone takes you shopping, buys tickets to the theater, and makes sure that your nights are filled with ecstasy! None of this costs you a cent. And they even buy farewell gifts for you and your family."

"All this has happened to you?" asks his companion.

"Well, not to me, but it happened to my wife."

✫ ✫ ✫

An old Jew meets an immigrant from Russia:

"It took me many years of living here before I discovered the best way to make a small fortune in Tel Aviv."

"And what is that?" asks the immigrant, all ears.

"Come here with a large fortune."

✫ ✫ ✫

A reporter is covering the arrival of a planeload of immigrants from Russia. He sees an old man with the beard of a patriarch, and runs up to him for his interview.

"Will you please answer a few questions?" he pleads. The old man consents. "What's the present state of the Russian economy?"

"I can't complain…"

"How are things in industry, agriculture, education?"

"I can't complain."

"What about anti-Semitism and human rights?"

"I can't complain."

If all that is true" says the reporter, "why did you emigrate?"

"Because here I can complain!"

✫ ✫ ✫

A client enters a grocery store in post-war Poland.
 "Any eggs?"
 "Not one."
 "Maybe some herrings?"
 "No."
 "Bread?"
 "Not a crumb."
 "Vodka?"
 "Not a drop.'"
 "Then do you have anything at all?"
 "Arthritis."

✡ ✡ ✡

A pauper strolls down a street, musing:
 "If I were rich, I would buy myself some clothes: a few suits, a warm coat for the winter, smart trousers for the summer, and comfortable shoes."
 He lifts his eyes to heaven and says:
 "Lord, you can do anything. Why not make a little miracle? I would be happy with a modest 500 shekels, though 1,000 shekels would be even better. It's no big thing for you."
 So engrossed, he slips on a banana skin and falls. Then, looking up again he says:
 "Don't make the miracle if you don't want to, but there's no need to knock me down."

An elderly lady brings a lapdog with her on a bus, and the driver asks whether she has a ticket for the dog.

"And if I buy a ticket, will it be allowed to sit like any passenger?"

"Of course," says the driver, "as long as it keeps its feet off the seat."

✭ ✭ ✭

A billboard outside a cafe in Tel Aviv proclaims that here, tourists can talk in many languages: English, German, French, Spanish, Russian, etc.

A young tourist comes in and asks the manager something in English. The manager waves his arms to say that he doesn't understand. The young man tries German, French, and Russian. At last, losing his patience he says in halting Hebrew:

"How could you hang out that bill board in front of the cafe?"

"In this café it is the tourists who speak many languages, not the owners."

✭ ✭ ✭

A newly arrived immigrant decides to buy a shop in Jerusalem. The owner encourages him eagerly:

"You should buy it. I lived here for thirty years. The shop is worth a gold mine." Some months later, the new owner meets the old one and says reproachfully:

"You cheated me! What was all this talk about a gold mine? Not even a dog came since I bought your shop."

"Every word was true. When I was the owner, it cost a gold mine to stay here."

✭ ✭ ✭

Four explorers are flying over Africa: an Englishman, a Frenchman, a German and an Israeli. The engine fails and they land deep in the jungle. They have no contact with the outside world, and they live only with wild animals. Much later, another expedition finds them and takes them back to Europe.

On their return, they all try to share their experience with others.

The German starts writing a multi-volume study titled *The Elephants And Their Culture*. The Frenchman writes a cycle of soft porn novels, *Sex Among the Elephants*. The Englishman gives a stirring speech in Parliament about *The Kingdom of the Elephants*, describing the new territories which he discovered for the Crown. The Israeli, on the other hand, tours the world giving lectures about *The Elephants and the Jewish Question*.

✫ ✫ ✫

A husband is reading the paper. He lifts his head and says: "Riva, did you read the statistics of motor accidents?"

"Here in Israel?"

"No, all over the world. Did you know, for instance, that in New York one pedestrian is hit by a car every twenty minutes?"

"That's terrible. The poor fellow has no luck at all. But why isn't he more careful?"

✫ ✫ ✫

Oprah has found a new job. The boss reminds her that her job is so sensitive, that it can only be entrusted to someone responsible.

"You're in luck," says Oprah. Things were always going wrong in my last firm, And whenever that happened, everyone said that I was responsible."

✫ ✫ ✫

A director is touring the offices of a government department. He stops by a clerk who is sitting in front of a wide open window.

"You could catch a cold in such weather," he says.

"Not likely," replies the clerk. "I'm used to sleeping with the window open."

✮ ✮ ✮

A bride-to-be asks one of her friends:

"What present did your fiancée buy you before your wedding?"

"Do you see that blue Cadillac parked in front of the house?"

"I see it."

"Do you like the color?"

"Very much."

"It's not too bright?"

"No."

"Or too dark?"

"No, it is altogether fabulous."

"Well, my fiancée bought me a scarf that was exactly the same color."

✮ ✮ ✮

A young woman asks her neighbor from across the road:

"Is someone ill in your house?"

"No, why do you ask?"

"Because I saw that handsome young doctor leaving your home at three o'clock in the morning."

"What of it? When I saw a soldier sneaking out of your house last Monday morning, did I ask you if this was the start of World War III?"

✮ ✮ ✮

A man is waiting to cross the main street in Tel Aviv. He stands and stands, but these are peak hours. The traffic lights are not working, and no one will let him through. Suddenly, he sees an old friend in the crowd on the other side of the road.

"Hey!" he shouts, "How did you do it?"

"Do what?"

"How did you cross to the other side?"

"I didn't cross. I was born here."

Levi is in a theater, trying to hear the dialog on the stage. A young couple behind him, obviously in love, are cooing sweet nothings to each other, and poor Levi is distracted.

"Please, I cannot hear a single word," he pleads.

"Really!" replies the girl. "Stop being nosy. If we wanted you to hear, we would have raised our voices."

✭ ✭ ✭

Two friends meet on the street:

"Good morning!"

"Good morning .."
"What's new?"
"Everything's..."
"And your job?"
"I can't ...."
"The kids ok?"
"They ..."
"That's great! Take care! See ya!"
"Bye! Let's keep in touch!"

✶ ✶ ✶

An official comes to the home of Rabinovitch during a census.
"How many children do you have?"
"Rivka, Moshe, Dani, Deborah, Rina, Uri! Children, gather round!"
"But comrade, this isn't necessary. All you need to do is to give me their numbers."
"No need to be sarcastic," says the mother. "I know we have a lot of children but, thank God, we still have enough names. We don't need to number them!"

✶ ✶ ✶

During a visit, there is a discussion about painting. The hostess turns to one of the guests and asks:
"Do you know Monet well?"
"Intimately," replies the woman. I met him yesterday on the 52 bus, the one that goes to Gorki Boulevard." There is an embarrassing silence, which lasts a long time.
The woman's husband turns to her on the way home: "People will laugh at us now. Everybody knows that the 52 bus doesn't go near Gorki."

✶ ✶ ✶

The constant devaluation of the Israeli shekel is the subject of many jokes.

An American cosmonaut lands on Mars, and is amazed to find an Israeli who is just planting a flag with the Star of David on top of a hill.

"How did you get here?" he cries. "

"I rose with the prices."

"But how will you come down back to Earth?"

"I will fall with the shekel!"

✡ ✡ ✡

Three friends meet in a cafe in Tel Aviv, on Friday afternoon, to talk and play cards. One is a surgeon, the second an architect, and third a politician. They wonder which is the oldest profession.

"Remember that God created Eve from Adam's rib. That was surgery."

"Agreed, but God created the Earth out of Chaos. Surely that was architecture!"

"And who do you think created Chaos?!" asks the politician.

✡ ✡ ✡

A distant cousin of the Goldfarb family writes to say that he will soon visit Israel, so uncle Goldfarb sits down and writes a reply.

"Dear cousin. We are very happy to learn that we will see you soon. Our son Dani was only two years old when you were last here. He is almost a young man now. How time flies! So bring a present for him, a Sharp's tape recorder for example. Hold it in your hand like an identity card, otherwise we will not be able to recognize you."

✡ ✡ ✡

A pious old Jew comes to Tel Aviv. He's surprised to see two Jews smoking in the hotel restaurant, and asks the receptionist:

"Do you see that? They're smoking on the Sabbath!"

"Oh, in Israel we don't worry about such trifles. Here smoking is a pleasure, not a sin".

A little later, he sees two men get into a car.

"They are going to travel on the Sabbath?"

"Where's the harm? They're going to a picnic, not to work. Pleasure's not a sin."

The old man is so shocked, that he asks for a whisky and some water to steady his nerves.

"To dilute such whisky with water would be a sin!" cries the receptionist.

"Thank God that you recognize at least one sin in Tel Aviv!"

✡ ✡ ✡

"Why do Jews reply to questions from others with questions of their own?"

"Why not?"

✡ ✡ ✡

21

From My Father

An old Jew enters a Polish delicatessen and buys some candy for his grandsons. But then his eyes start to caress the shelves hung with rings of aromatic kielbasas, mounds of kabanos, and whole pyramids of hams. The aroma of these meats torments him until he can stand it no longer.

"Please give me half a kilo of that smoked salmon," he points.

"But that's not salmon, sir, that's lean krakowska ham." says the sales assistant.

"Oh, and who asked for your opinion?"

✯ ✯ ✯

Two opera impresarios clash in court. Max Rigelbloom accuses:

"Your Honor, my opponent Fritz Pupke has turned the head of my star soprano. He is a seducer, a scoundrel and a liar!

"Your Honor, how can you allow my opponent to insult me like this?" cries Pupke.

"Mister Rigelbloom, until your case is proven you must withdraw your insults.

"As you wish. your Honor. Rigelbloom then shouts with challenging scorn:

"Fritz Pupke is NOT a scoundrel?, he is NOT a liar?'

"Your Honor, he is still insulting me!"

"What do you want, your Honor, the libretto or the melody?

✯ ✯ ✯

Moses Cohen is hit by a drunken lord driving a Rolls Royce in London. The judge penalizes the lord with stiff compensations of one million pounds. Moses looks content, but the Ace Insurance agent feels that Moses is only pretending that he cannot walk.

"You don't need your wheel chair! I will follow you and catch you," he says.

"Thank you, dear sir" smiles Moses. "I plan to see the world. How nice of you to share my journey. I hope you can afford it. We will travel first class of course, stay only in five-star hotels, and eat in the best restaurants. I will start with Rome, where my ancestors built the amphitheater. Then Egypt where Jews worked in bondage. Then, on to Masada in Israel, where I will be carried up that mountain where many faint with fatigue. India with tiger hunts from elephants is next, and I hope you can stomach those red-hot curries. I want to visit Everest, where Sherpas will carry me, while you enjoy your stroll to the base camp at 18,000 feet. Next, at the Great Wall of China, I will have rickshaws while you follow. Then, just before the money runs out, I will go to Lourdes, famous as the scene of many faith healings. And there, my friend, you will witness a miracle!"

Yankel is decorated for exceptional valor in World War I. On two occasions, when on sentry duty, alone, at night, in the depth of winter, he penetrated the trenches of the enemy, and seized their battle standards. When asked what drove him to these acts of heroism, he answered modestly that he did it for his great love of Russia and the Tsar. He is basking in the admiration of his colleagues, when a friend asks:

"Yankel, I never imagined that you were such a hero!"

"What hero? They always gave me the watch on Sunday nights, so that they could drink and sleep in peace. You know those long, cold Russian nights. I stamped my feet and sang old Yiddish folk songs my mother taught me. One night, a soldier called out from the other side that he also knew those songs. It was my cousin Moriz, who was pressed into the German army when on a trading trip. We soon got sore throats shouting to each other across no-man's land, so we started to visit each other, just to be together and talk about old times. And, you know, it's always nice to bring a present on a visit, so he would bring one of their flags, and I would bring one of ours."

✯ ✯ ✯

A Polish nobleman, traveling in his carriage, meets a Jew on the road and asks: "Where are you from, my man?"

"From Vilna" The Jew replies.

The nobleman, seeing that the Jew doesn't show the expected signs of respect for a grandee by bowing and taking off his hat, shakes his cane at him and shouts:

"The hat! The hat!"

"Also from Vilna."

✯ ✯ ✯

"What's purple, hangs on a wall, and squeals when pressed with a finger?"
"I give up!"
"A herring!"
"How can it be a herring? A herring's not purple!"
"Well, someone painted this herring purple."
"But herrings don't hang on walls!"
"Well, someone hung this herring on a wall."
"But a dead herring does not squeal when you press it with a finger."
"True, I had to put that in to make this puzzle more difficult to solve."

✧ ✧ ✧

Two social-climbing friends have just visited a cultured couple of society leaders. One of the friends keeps gushing with admiration for the good taste of their hosts:

"Sarah, did you see their exquisite antique furniture?"

But Sarah sticks her nose in the air: "Phi, we can afford to buy new furniture!"

✧ ✧ ✧

Wealthy Polish. landowner Sigmund Dolega and merchant Isaak Goldblum have just concluded a very satisfying deal, and are celebrating in Dolega's manor. They both enjoy the carp in mushroom sauce. Later, a roasted suckling pig is served with the finest old vodka, and Goldblum doesn't touch either.

"What's wrong?" asks Dolega. "You scorn Polish hospitality!?"

"Not at all, but our Scriptures forbid us to eat pork, and to drink hard liquor."

"They forbid it even when you are starving?

"Well, we would be allowed to eat it only if it was a matter of life or death."

At this "Dolega springs to his feet and reaches for one of the ancient sabers that hang on his wall, raises it above Goldblum's head and cries:

"Eat and drink up, or else!"

Goldblum doesn't lose his dignity or composure. He loads up his plate, and munches silently. He takes a second helping of crackling, drains three glasses of vodka, smacks his lips and says: "Did you really have to wait so long to grab that saber?"

✡ ✡ ✡

A young Russian Jew is leaving for Israel, and agrees that his uncle will write every year to report how things are going. If things are bad, he will write in red ink. One year later, the emigrant gets his first letter:

"Things could not be better. Under the inspired guidance of our Party, life is a constant joy. The shops would amaze you with the profusion and quality of the caviar and smoked salmon. Our clothing is stylish and elegant, and shops are full of merchandise. In fact, the only thing that is difficult to get is red ink."

✡ ✡ ✡

Great pianist Ignaz Friedman told this story about his mother:

"Ignaz my son, before I die, I give you this advice: take, always take. Take whatever they give you, no matter what it is, even if it's just a cabbage leaf or a piece of string. But if anyone wants to take from you, call the police!"

✡ ✡ ✡

Glossary

Balagula	Cart driver
Chassid	Pious believer in joyful worship
Cheder	Old-style orthodox Hebrew school
Chazan	Cantor
Goy	A Gentile, Non Jewish.
Klezmer	A Jewish folk musician, and music.
Kosher	Food prepared according to Jewish dietary laws.
Mamele	Mummy (Dear little mama}
Melamed	Itinerant teacher in Hebrew school
Maggid	Preacher
Rabbi (Rebbe}	Teacher, respected scholar, spiritual leader
Sabbath	From sunset on Friday to sunset on Saturday
Shadchan	Marriage broker
Shammes	Sexton or caretaker of a synagogue
Shtetl	Small town with strong Jewish presence
Talmud	Teachings interpreting Scripture
Torah	Jewish Scriptures. The five books of Moses
Yarmulke	Skull cap
Yeshiva	Talmudic college

This book's jokes and characters are works of humor and fiction. Any and all references to people, places, and events in the book are fictional. Any resemblance to real people or places or events is purely coincidental.

www.ingramcontent.com/pod-product-compliance
Lightning Source LLC
Chambersburg PA
CBHW081013040426
42444CB00014B/3195